AROUND san francisco WITH KIDS

2nd Edition

by Clark Norton

Fodor's Travel Publications
New York • Toronto • London • Sydney • Auckland

www.fodors.com

CREDITS

Writer: Clark Norton
Series Editors: Karen Cure, Andrea Lehman
Editor: Andrea Lehman
Editorial Production: Marina Padakis
Production/Manufacturing: Robert Shields

Design: Fabrizio La Rocca, *creative director;*
Tigist Getachew, *art director*
Illustration and Series Design: Rico Lins, Keren Ora
Admoni/Rico Lins Studio

ABOUT THE WRITER

Clark Norton, author of *Fodor's Where Should We Take the Kids?: California*, writes about family travel for *Family Fun*, *Family Life*, *Parenting*, and *ParentCenter.com*. His articles have won two Gold Awards from the Pacific Asia Travel Association. He has two children, son Grael and daughter Lia, both born and reared in San Francisco.

ISBN 0-679-00916-7
ISSN 1526-1395
Second Edition

Although all prices, opening times, and other details in this book are based on information supplied to us at press time, changes occur all the time in the travel world, and Fodor's cannot accept responsibility for facts that become outdated or for inadvertent errors or omissions. So always confirm information when it matters, especially if you're making a detour to visit a specific place.

SPECIAL SALES

Fodor's Travel Publications are available at special discounts for bulk purchases for sales promotions or premiums. Special editions, including personalized covers, excerpts of existing guides, and corporate imprints, can be created in large quantities for special needs. For more information, contact your local bookseller or Special Markets, Fodor's Travel Publications, 280 Park Avenue, New York, NY 10017. Inquiries from Canada should be directed to your local Canadian bookseller or sent to Random House of Canada, Ltd., Marketing Dept., 2775 Matheson Boulevard East, Mississauga, Ontario L4W 4P7. Inquiries from the United Kingdom should be sent to Fodor's Travel Publications, 20 Vauxhall Bridge Road, London, England SW1V 2SA.

PRINTED IN THE UNITED STATES OF AMERICA
10 9 8 7 6 5 4 3 2 1

COUNTDOWN TO GOOD TIMES

GET READY, GET SET!

Between drop-offs, pickups, and after-school activities, organizing your family's schedule can seem like a full-time job. Planning for some fun time together shouldn't have to be another. That's where this book helps out. We've done all the legwork, so you don't have to. Open to any page and you'll find a great family activity in the San Francisco Bay Area already planned out. You can read about the main events—most within San Francisco or a short drive away (none more than 90 minutes from the city)—check our age-appropriateness ratings to make sure it's right for your family, pick up some insider tips, and find out where to grab a bite nearby.

To suit most any family's interests and needs, we've included a balance of attractions. You'll find things to do indoors and out, destinations that range from world famous to off the beaten path, events that will fill a day or just a few hours, and activities that appeal to a variety of ages (including parents!). Most of the 68 things to do are available year-round, though some are seasonal (days and hours are listed). And though some of the places, such as theme parks, will take a crunch from your wallet, many others are inexpensive—or even free.

HOW TO SAVE MONEY
Taking a family on an outing can be pricey, but there are ways to save.

1. Think beyond theme parks. While an amusement or theme park can be a great treat, you can have plenty of fun with your kids without dropping $40 a head. The Bay Area has priceless natural treasures—such as Muir Woods National Monument and Point

Reyes National Seashore—that cost little or nothing to visit. Urban parks (such as San Francisco's Golden Gate Park or Presidio National Park) are other great bargains, as are historic sites, wildlife refuges, and many museums.

2. Watch for discounts, coupons, and passes. Ask about discounts at ticket booths; your affiliation (and an ID) may get you a break. Consider buying season passes. At some theme parks, they may cost only as much as two or three one-day admissions. Many attractions also give discounts for consecutive-day visits or for buying combination tickets to sister attractions (such as Six Flags Marine World and Waterworld USA). Family memberships to some institutions pay off if you visit more than once or twice. Coupons, meanwhile, can save you up to $4 a ticket at certain attractions; look for them in hotels, supermarkets, government tourism offices, even your pediatrician's office. Also watch for special tourist-oriented passes such as CityPass ($33.75 for adults, $24.75 for children ages 5–17), which will save you about half off at five San Francisco attractions (you must visit all within nine days), as well as provide a one-week unlimited Muni transit pass, which includes cable cars.

3. Try to go on free days. Several places in this book (such as the California Academy of Sciences, California Palace of the Legion of Honor, the Exploratorium, and the San Francisco Museum of Modern Art) offer free admission on certain days of the week or month.

4. Pack a lunch. These are perfect for parks and natural areas, but even theme parks set space aside for do-it-yourself picnics. You can always buy treats to supplement what you bring.

GOOD TIMING
Most attractions with kid appeal are busiest when school is out. If you have preschool kids, try to tour crowded attractions (such as Alcatraz Island) on weekdays or in the off-season. If you want to go on a holiday, call ahead, as we list only regular operating hours. It's always a good idea to call ahead anyway, particularly if you're making a special trip. Attractions sometimes change their hours or close unexpectedly.

The weather also plays a role in good timing. San Francisco has an unusual weather pattern that catches many out-of-towners by surprise. Summertime can actually be one of the coolest seasons in the city, since that's when fog often blankets the bay. Anytime you set out for a day in the Bay Area, dress in layers. What can start out as a bright, sunny day can turn windy and cold before you can count to 10 goose bumps. The closer you get to the ocean, on the way seeing sights such as the Cliff House, Ft. Funston, Ocean Beach, and the San Francisco Zoo, the better your chances of encountering fog.

OTHER SOURCES OF INFORMATION
The San Francisco Convention and Visitors Bureau (tel. 415/391–2000; www.sfvisitor.org) has a Visitor Information Center on the lower level of Hallidie

Plaza (900 Market St., at Powell St.) in downtown San Francisco. Along with brochures and maps, you can pick up coupons and Muni transit passes. Hours are weekdays 8:30–5, weekends 9–3. There's also an official California Welcome Center office at San Francisco's Pier 39.

TRANSPORTATION

Even if you have a car, traffic and parking woes around crowded tourist attractions often make it unwise to drive. Mass transit alternatives include cable cars, buses, and streetcars. You can buy one-, three-, and seven-day adult passports for unlimited rides on Muni—including cable cars—for $6, $10, and $15, respectively (children ages 5–17 pay reduced prices anyway). Call 415/673–6864 for Muni information. You can also get connected to operators at just about any Bay Area transit office by calling 415/817–1717, the travelers information system.

MORE THINGS TO DO

Even a list of 68 activities can't cover everything there is to do with kids in the Bay Area. Watch for seasonal arts programs, such as the San Francisco Ethnic Dance Festival (tel. 415/474–3914), which takes place each June and hosts dance troupes representing cultures around the globe, as well as special family concerts presented by the San Francisco Symphony (tel. 415/864–6000). The Greater Bay Area has a number of state parks ideal for a visit with kids, including Big Basin Redwood State Park (tel. 831/338–8860), with great hiking north of Santa Cruz; Tomales Bay State Park (tel. 415/669–1140), which has gentle beaches near Point Reyes National Seashore; Samuel P. Taylor State

Park (tel. 415/488-9897), also in Marin County, where you can camp; Jack London State Historic Park (tel. 707/938-5216), in Sonoma County, where the famed adventure writer lived the last days of his life; and Fort Ross State Historic Park (tel. 707/847-3286), on the Sonoma Coast, where you can see remnants of a 19th-century Russian outpost.

SAFETY CATCH
Whenever you travel with kids, take a few sensible precautions. Show them how to recognize staff or security people when you arrive at an attraction. Designate a meeting time and place in case you become separated. Keep a close eye on young children at all times—especially at Bay Area beaches, which have strong waves, rip currents, and undertow.

FINAL THOUGHTS
We'd love to hear yours: What did you and your kids think about the places we recommend? Have you found other places we should include? Send us your ideas via e-mail (c/o editors@fodors.com, specifying Around San Francisco with Kids on the subject line) or snail mail (c/o Around San Francisco With Kids, Fodor's Travel Publications, 280 Park Avenue, New York, NY 10017). Meanwhile, have a great day around San Francisco with your kids!

Clark Norton

ALCATRAZ ISLAND

The maximum-security prison on Alcatraz, closed in 1963, once held some of the nation's most incorrigible criminals—and though it's just 1¼ miles and a 10-minute boat ride from Fisherman's Wharf, the 12-acre island still seems eerily isolated, its lighthouse tower often shrouded in mist. Over the past 150 years, the Rock has been a fortification, military prison, federal penitentiary, and site of an American Indian occupation. But since becoming a national park in 1973, Alcatraz has also become one of San Francisco's most popular tourist sites. Its reputation as "America's Devil's Island" and its gorgeous views are irresistible lures.

Hop one of the Blue & Gold Fleet ferries, the only public transport to the island, and be sure to dress warmly and wear comfortable shoes—the island terrain is rocky and sometimes steep. Once here, you and your kids can peer into the tiny, spartan cells that once held the likes of Al Capone, Machine Gun Kelly, and Robert ("Birdman of Alcatraz") Stroud, and visit the grim "dark holes" where disobedient prisoners were left to languish by themselves

HEY, KIDS! Can you imagine a bunch of man-eating sharks circling Alcatraz? That's what prison wardens and guards told inmates to scare them out of trying to escape. Actually, there were—and are—no dangerous sharks. In 1962, three prisoners did tunnel out with sharpened spoons. Though they made it off the island, they weren't seen again, so no one knows if they reached shore alive. This tale became the basis of *Escape From Alcatraz*, one of several films set in the island prison.

Departures: Pier 41, Fisherman's Wharf

415/773–1188 schedule, 415/705–5555 ferry, 415/705–1042 park; www.nps.gov/alcatraz

Tours $8.75–$19.75 ages 12 and up, $5.50–$10.50 children 5–11

Boats daily 9:30–4:15; also evenings, call for times

5 and up

in total darkness. Other sights include the mess hall (complete with the last day's menu), the library, and the exercise yard, where catwalks and guard towers loomed overhead. From the concrete bleachers, prisoners could glimpse the gleaming city across the bay and smell the coffee roasting in North Beach. Surprisingly, although Alcatraz could hold 450 prisoners, no more than 250 were ever incarcerated at a time, and barely a tenth that number were here at the end.

Choose between taking a self-guided tour, using an audiocassette or pamphlet, or going with a ranger. School-age kids are often riveted by the Cell House Audio Tour, which includes ex-inmates and guards describing their experiences. When it's open—usually September–January, depending on bird-nesting season—the Agave Trail, along the island's southern rim, makes for a great short hike. A visit to Alcatraz lasts 2–3 hours, but chances are your kids will remember the details for years to come.

KEEP IN MIND

Start your visit to Alcatraz early. The ferries hold 300 people per sailing, so advance boat reservations are strongly advised and are essential in summer or on holiday weekends throughout the year. Call or stop by the Pier 41 ticket window at least two weeks ahead.

EATS FOR KIDS You can picnic around the Alcatraz dock but not beyond it—not an ideal arrangement—and there are no eateries on the island. The **Jail House Cafe** (Pier 41) is a small take-out place just to the right of the Blue & Gold Fleet ticket booth; here you can get a hot dog, burger, or bowl of clam chowder while waiting for the boat. At the **Eagle Café** (Pier 39, tel. 415/433–3689), load up on big breakfasts and lunches in an old-time waterfront atmosphere.

ANGEL ISLAND STATE PARK

Want to escape with your kids to an island park where the air is fresh, cars are banned, and grassy picnic areas, rocky coves, forested slopes, and 13 miles of hiking and biking trails await? Angel Island, the largest island in San Francisco Bay, is just a 40-minute ferry ride from Fisherman's Wharf.

The fun begins on the Blue & Gold Fleet ferry ride across the bay (dress in layers, since the ride can get chilly). Once on the island, you can spread out a blanket or grab a picnic table at Ayala Cove, not far from the ferry dock, where there's plenty of grass, shade, and a small beach. Waters are cold and often rough and not meant for swimming, though, and there are no lifeguards. But lots of families hang out at the cove all day, tossing Frisbees or playing volleyball.

Alternatively, you can set off on a hiking or biking trip, best for kids ages 8 and up. The easiest route is the paved-and-gravel, mostly level, 5-mile Perimeter Road, which rings

EATS FOR KIDS Many families bring a picnic. The **Cove Café** (tel. 415/897–0715), near the island ferry dock, serves sandwiches, salads, and soups on a harbor-view deck; the café is open daily May–October, with limited days March–April and November. For restaurants near Pier 41, see #68.

HEY, KIDS! In the early part of the last century, 1910–1940, Angel Island was used as an entry station for 175,000 Asians (mostly Chinese) who were immigrating to America. It was the first place they stayed when they arrived in the United States. Most left the island after a few weeks, but some were held for months or even years. You can visit the barracks where they lived on the eastern side of the island. Look for the poems they carved into the dormitory walls. Many of the poems are sad because their authors missed their homes and families.

the entire island and offers 360° views of the bay. You can either bring your own bike or, from spring to fall, rent one near the dock ($10 per hour, $30 per day). If exercise doesn't appeal, a one-hour narrated tram tour ($7.50-$11.50) covers much of the territory. Hikers can also climb to the top of the island on fairly narrow and steep dirt trails, recommended for kids 10 and older. If you go hiking, have the kids keep an eye out for such animals as deer and raccoons, hawks and pelicans, and, just offshore, sea lions and harbor seals.

The island has nine hike-in campsites (tel. 800/444-7275; $7). Sites 1-4 are best for small groups. Bring charcoal or a camp stove and prepare to haul equipment for 1 or 2 miles. But however you choose to spend your day (or night) on Angel Island, you'll find it offers one of the great escapes from San Francisco—without ever leaving the city limits.

KEEP IN MIND Paying attention to the calendar—and your watch— can make a trip to Angel Island more pleasant. May and September tend to be less foggy and less congested than the summer months. Ferry and other services are limited from November to April. If you're bringing a bike, get to the ferry early; bike passage is limited and first-come, first-served. And unless you want to make an unexpected camping trip, allow plenty of time to catch the last ferry back to San Francisco.

This reserve just off Highway 1, about 55 miles south of San Francisco, is home to one of California's great natural spectacles. Each winter, more than 4,000 massive Northern elephant seals come ashore to the beaches here to rest, mate, and give birth. Once nearly extinct, these protected marine mammals have staged a remarkable comeback, breeding successfully on Año Nuevo for more than 40 years.

The elephant seals spend much of their year out in the Pacific and in feeding grounds along British Columbia, Canada, to the north. The enormous males, weighing up to 3,000 pounds, are the first to return to Año Nuevo each December, battling each other for dominance in ferocious displays of raw power. The females, who weigh up to a ton, arrive around New Year's and give birth a few days later. Watching the newborn pups struggle to survive is a moving experience. Meanwhile, the adults mate again, usually in less than a month, and then head out to sea by mid-March, leaving the pups to learn to swim by themselves. By late April, the pups head north to Canada to feed. Older

KEEP IN MIND Año Nuevo may be a state reserve, but this is no walk in the park. Evaluate your kids' tolerance for discomfort and their maturity levels. Getting within 40 feet of elephant seals can be dangerous, so hold hands with young kids. Carry very small children in a backpack or front pack (no strollers). Dress for possible cold and windy weather and muddy terrain, and bring rain ponchos, since walks leave rain or shine and umbrellas aren't permitted. Allow up to 1½ hours to make the drive from San Francisco; late arrivals lose their reservations. Leave pets at home.

elephant seals return to molt from April to August, and yearling seals are often seen here in fall.

From mid-December to March the public is allowed to visit the breeding grounds only on naturalist-led guided walks, which cover 3 miles and last about 2½ hours. Reservations are essential and can be made starting in late October, up to eight weeks in advance. From April through November, free first-come, first-served permits to visit the elephant seal grounds are issued daily (8:30–3:30); allow 2–3 hours for the hike. The reserve covers a wild, undeveloped coastal point of windswept dunes and rocky offshore islands, and in addition to the elephant seals, you can view a prolific assortment of sea lions, harbor seals, sea otters, offshore gray whales, and shorebirds. So even if you don't come for the guided walks, you may witness natural wonders at Año Nuevo most any time of year.

EATS FOR KIDS
No food or beverages are sold at the reserve, but picnic tables are available. The nearest town, Pescadero, is the site of venerable **Duarte's Tavern** (202 Stage Rd., tel. 650/879–0464), known for its artichoke soup, seafood, and homemade pies, but kids can also get PB&Js.

HEY, KIDS! Since elephant seals weigh up to 1½ tons, you know they must have hearty appetites. When they're feeding at sea, they dive as far as 2,000 feet down and feast on ratfish, skates, rays, squid, and small sharks. Yum! But here's what's interesting: The females eat nothing at all while they're mating, giving birth, and nursing their pups, and even the males mostly stop eating at that time. It's kind of like nature's version of Weight Watchers.

AQUARIUM OF THE BAY

65

Formerly called UnderWater World, the Aquarium of the Bay bills itself as America's first "diver's-eye view" aquarium, though others have opened since. Here you and your children walk in clear acrylic tunnels to view an array of sharks, bat rays, eels, sturgeon, sea stars, and other creatures that dwell in San Francisco Bay. The concept is an intriguing one: People are, in effect, on the inside looking out into the tanks, while the marine life—swimming freely above and around the humans—are on the outside looking in.

Despite its prime location at Pier 39 (*see* #18), the aquarium has encountered financial problems and struggled to draw locals, many of whom view it primarily as a tourist attraction—or trap. It also faces tough competition from other area aquariums, such as the Steinhart Aquarium in Golden Gate Park (*see* #39). The name change and a new emphasis on interactivity—including more naturalists available to answer questions—are intended to lure more Bay Area visitors.

HEY, KIDS!
See how many different shark species you can spot (hint: there are seven). Look for leopard sharks (with spots), spiny dogfish sharks (long and thin), six-gill sharks (count the gills), seven-gill sharks (ditto), plus smooth hound, Pacific angel, and soupfin sharks—sorry, no more clues!

KEEP IN MIND The aquarium can be enjoyable and educational, but a family of four could easily spend $1 a minute or more for the experience. Factor in the well-stocked gift shop, which you enter when you "resurface." Loaded with undersea-related merchandise ranging from books and jewelry to sweatshirts and stuffed sharks, it's bound to catch your kids' eyes. (Just try to get out without some shark or other taking a bite out of your wallet.) And that's not counting all the other ways to blow your budget on Pier 39. So consider the cost before taking the plunge.

Beach St. at the Embarcadero

 $12.95 ages 12 and up,
$6.50 children 3–11

Daily 9–8

 415/623–5300, 888/732–3483;
www.aquariumofthebay.com

3 and up

Many families love what they see during their "dive into the bay" (actually an elevator descent, but dramatic license is allowed). Two 400-foot-long transparent tunnels usher you "into" a two-story tank that holds more than 700,000 gallons of water and 16,000 sea creatures. When you spot a shark swimming directly over your head—well, that's an experience not easily forgotten.

Narration, played on headphones while you ride a slow-moving walkway, is jaunty and informative. You can get off the walkway if you wish to stroll at your own pace or linger for a spell. Figure 30–40 minutes to complete your "dive." (It's a bit awkward taking strollers on the moving walkway, and kids need to be age 6 or so to fully appreciate the headphone narration, though young children can certainly admire all those fish.) Later, kids get a chance to touch sea stars, sea urchins, and other creatures in a shallow tank. But what do the fish—without benefit of headphones—think of all those humans passing by? We can only watch and wonder.

EATS FOR KIDS If the Aquarium of the Bay gets you hungry for seafood, the **Bubba Gump Shrimp Co. Restaurant** (Pier 39, tel. 415/781–4867), themed after the film *Forrest Gump,* has it. (Hint: go for the shrimp, served at least 10 ways.) Another seafood option is **Pier Market** (Pier 39, tel. 415/989–7437), which dishes up mesquite-grilled fresh fish and good clam chowder. For information on the **Sea Lion Café,** the **Burger Cafe,** the **Eagle Café,** and other choices in the area, see #68, #43, #38, and #18.

ARDENWOOD HISTORIC FARM

When was the last time your kids got to pump water, crank an old clothes wringer, or plant some crops? If the only hands-on activity they've gotten lately is hitting the button on the remote control, then head for the antidote for urban couch potatodom: Ardenwood Historic Farm. In southern Alameda County and part of the East Bay Regional Park District, Ardenwood is *the* place to introduce city children to life on a real working farm— a 19th-century farm at that. At this 200-acre complex, your kids—and you—can join in the pumping and cranking that were required to keep a farm going back in the Victorian age, and even help feed the livestock and plant, tend, and harvest the crops.

You can watch as costumed docents give farm-chore and craft making demonstrations, such as horseshoe hammering, hay harvesting, lace-making, barrel-making, and biscuit baking. As on any farm, the activities change from season to season and even week to week; what you see and do in spring will be quite different from in the fall.

KEEP IN MIND To maintain the old-time atmosphere, Ardenwood doesn't allow anyone to bring modern play equipment onto the grounds. This includes electronic games and any contemporary sporting equipment, such as Frisbees, footballs, and soccer balls. It's okay to carry in adult "toys" (cameras, video cameras, cell phones, and the like), but if you really want to get into the spirit of things, you may want to turn your phone off. And though dogs were definitely around during the 19th century, they're not permitted at Ardenwood. Arf!

Ardenwood dates from the days following the 1849 Gold Rush, when a failed gold prospector named George Washington Patterson established a ranch here. Patterson's restored farmhouse and Victorian gardens are still on view, and you can take free tours of the house on a first-come, first-served basis. But most kids under 10 would find the tours a yawn, though they'd jump at the chance to take a horse-drawn hay wagon or horse-drawn train ride, both included in admission (except on Saturdays, when they aren't available). Plenty of other farm animals are on hand, too, including sheep, goats, pigs, chickens, bunnies, turkeys, and cows.

Ardenwood hosts a variety of special events, which cost $1.50–$2.50 extra: old-fashioned Fourth of July and Christmas celebrations, summer and fall harvest festivals, concerts, and re-creations of Victorian-era social occasions. By the time you've completed your visit to this living yet historical farm, your children might just realize that potatoes don't grow on couches.

GETTING THERE You can't reach the 19th century without some twists and turns. Take I–880 to the Dumbarton Bridge turnoff. Go west on Highway 84, and take the Ardenwood Boulevard exit. Turn right at the signal, and look for the Ardenwood sign.

EATS FOR KIDS Ardenwood has nice picnic areas (the grounds are also open Tuesdays and Wednesdays for picnics only). The **Farmyard Café** (tel. 510/797-5621) here sells hot dogs, ice cream, and, for special events, barbecued foods. In a small shopping plaza across from the park entrance, you'll find **Ardenwood Pizza and Games** (34765 Ardenwood Blvd., tel. 510/744-9900), where the pizza parlor is adjacent to batting cages, a go-cart track, and a mini golf course. Nearby, Newark's Jarvis Avenue is lined with fast-food places.

BASIC BROWN BEAR FACTORY

As the owners of this Potrero Hill factory put it, this is "a place where teddy bears are born." Since 1976, Merrilee and Eric Woods have been making teddy bears here, and since 1985, they've let kids help in assembling, stuffing, and "bathing" them. More than 65,000 Bay Area kids have done just that, and it's become one of the top child-oriented factory tours in the country.

Here's how it works: Basic Brown Bear provides the pattern, material, stuffing, and instructions for a cuddly toy. Your child helps put it together, deciding how chubby or slender it will be and whether or not to add beans to liven up the polyester fiberfill. Staff and stuffing machine are there to assist, too. In fact, a staff member helps sew up the bear and groom it, and your youngster provides the final touch with a blow-dry "bath." All you have to do is pay for it.

EATS FOR KIDS **San Francisco BBQ** (1328 18th St., tel. 415/431–8956) serves reasonably priced Thai barbecue (grilled chicken or beef) and noodle dishes in casual surroundings. **Sally's** (300 De Haro St., tel. 415/626–6006) is a breakfast-and-lunch spot known for great omelets, home fries, and baked goods like scones and muffins.

KEEP IN MIND Although you can tour the factory for free, the lure of seeing your children make their own bears—and the fear of disappointing them—is so great that few families emerge bear naked. If you don't want to risk your kids clamoring to take home costly Big Fred, call for a catalog before you visit, so you can preselect an appropriately priced bear. Your kids can also buy and stuff bears at a minibranch of Basic Brown Bear Factory at the Cannery shopping complex (2801 Leavenworth St., Fisherman's Wharf, tel. 415/931–6670), but this bear outpost doesn't give tours.

444 De Haro St., at Mariposa St.

 Free, bears $12–$999

 415/626–0781, 800/554–1910;
www.basicbrownbear.com

 M–Sa 10–5, Su 11–5; tours Su–F 1,
Sa 11 and 1

2–10

The cost of the teddy bears depends on the size and complexity of the patterns, all of which are designed by Merrilee Woods and made right at the factory. There are more than 40 styles of bear to choose from. The least expensive (and simplest pattern), Baby Bear, stands 13″ high and is priced at less than a dollar per inch. The biggest and most expensive, Big Fred, stands 6′ 8″ tall and costs nearly $1,000. A popular, moderately priced model, Gigi, costs $24. In addition, a full range of more than 70 outfits and accessories—dresses, tutus, jumpers, T-shirts, tuxedos, bridal outfits, vests, pants, surfer shirts, overalls, sleep shirts, sweaters, engineer outfits, and Nutcracker uniforms—are for sale.

The factory's free ½-hour drop-in tours demonstrate how the bears are designed, cut, and sewn. (These are geared to families or groups of eight or fewer; larger groups should call for reservations.) When all is said, done, and stuffed, your children will probably treasure these cuddly animals above others because they helped make them.

HEY, KIDS! Here are the bear facts about how the "teddy" got its name: A century ago, Theodore ("Teddy") Roosevelt, who was then president of the United States, was on a hunting trip in Mississippi. According to the story, he refused to shoot a helpless bear that others had caught and tied up to a tree. Someone drew a newspaper cartoon about it, and the story became famous. A New York shopkeeper then decided to name some stuffed bears his wife had made after the president. The man started selling the bears, and the rest, as they say, is history.

One of the state's top children's museums, the Bay Area Discovery Museum is housed in seven buildings that were once part of Ft. Baker, an Army post. Now part of the Golden Gate National Recreation Area, the site has knockout views of the Golden Gate Bridge, since the museum rests virtually below its northern end. But for most kids, the views take a distant second place to the buzz of activities inside—all sorts of hands-on learning adventures, which to the uninitiated can bear a striking resemblance to playing.

Appropriately, the bay's natural wonders provide one realm of discovery. In the Bay Hall, your kids can crawl through a tunnel "beneath" the sea or fish aboard their own Discovery Boat. In the Maze of Illusions, mirrors and holograms challenge perception of color, dimension, and distance. Other attractions include an interactive Media Center, where youngsters check out computer animation; a science lab focusing on local plants and animals; art and ceramics studios; and an architecture and design area. Toddlers have their own interactive discovery area—Tot Spot—where they can enter a storybook cave with adjustable

EATS FOR KIDS The museum's **Discovery Cafe** (tel. 415/289–7269) has indoor and outdoor seating and foods appealing to both kids (hot dogs, burgers, peanut butter and jelly sandwiches) and parents (sandwiches and salads with ingredients like goat cheese and sun-dried tomatoes). You can also picnic on the grounds. In downtown Sausalito, the creatively named **Hamburgers** (737 Bridgeway, tel. 415/332–9471) has, you guessed it, burgers and fries—plus fish-and-chips, hot dogs, and ice cream. Sit inside, where it's cramped, or get your food to go.

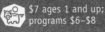

lighting and an echo chamber, or sit on a waterbed and watch live fish above. Special exhibits change every few months. Outside in a play area called Discovery Park, bridges, trucks, and boats await.

Half-hour weekday morning drop-in programs cater to toddlers and preschoolers. In Miss Kitty . . . Hop & Boogie Down by the Bay, kids learn dance, music, and creative movement, while in Bangin', Twangin', and Shakin', they sing, dance, and play instruments. Scribbles & Squiggles is all about art. Drop-in Saturday afternoon ceramics labs, by contrast, are for ages 5 and up. Kids might make a clay pot, figurine, or treasure box, all of which the teacher will fire in a kiln. Meanwhile, the museum's Discovery Store stocks educational and entertaining books, CD-ROMs, activity kits, and art supplies to take home. That may occupy them until your next visit here—which, if the kids have anything to say about it, may well come soon.

HEY, KIDS! Did you know that when you go to the Bay Area Discovery Museum, you're actually visiting a national park? The museum is the only children's museum in a national park in the whole country. Before that, the buildings here were part of an Army fort.

GETTING THERE The museum is off the beaten track, and roads are not well marked. Soon after crossing the Golden Gate Bridge north from San Francisco, take the Alexander Avenue exit off U.S. 101, going right toward Sausalito. Immediately get in the left-hand lane, and make your first left onto Bunker Road. Then make your first right and go down the hill. At the bottom, make a right at the stop sign (going around the parade ground), and make a left at the next stop sign. The museum is on the right-hand side on McReynolds Road.

A big part of the San Francisco Bay experience is getting out on the water, and kids are often among the most enthusiastic boat riders. Two of the most popular trips go to Alcatraz Island and Angel Island State Park (*see* #68 and #67), and, May–October, you can even combine the two in a one-day extravaganza offered by the Blue & Gold Fleet. But if you just want a boat trip without touring islands on the other end or if your timing isn't right for an Alcatraz or Angel Island trip, there's another good option: a one-hour bay cruise. Take your pick between the Blue & Gold Fleet, operating from Pier 39's west marina, and the Red & White Fleet, leaving from Pier 43½, at Fisherman's Wharf. The trips are similar, and the costs are the same.

The narrated cruises hit the bay highlights, providing unobstructed views from the water and offering a little history along the way. Leaving the wharf area, you'll get nice perspectives of the San Francisco waterfront and the skyline beyond, including

EATS FOR KIDS Cruise boats have small **snack bars** aboard, selling drinks, chips, and the like, but don't count on them for real meals. For eateries near the pier, such as the **Eagle Café**, **Alioto's**, and the **Burger Cafe**, see #68, #43, and #18.

KEEP IN MIND If you don't want to pay cruise boat prices, but you still want to get out on the water, ride a ferryboat instead. There's no narration, but the scenery's just as good. Blue & Gold Fleet runs ferries to Oakland's Jack London Square in the East Bay and to Sausalito and Tiburon in the North Bay, among other destinations. Golden Gate Ferry (tel. 415/923–2000), meanwhile, runs ferryboats to Sausalito and Larkspur, also in the North Bay. The Blue & Gold ferries leave from Pier 41 or the Ferry Building (the Embarcadero and Market St.); Golden Gate ferries leave from the Ferry Building.

Departures from Piers 39 and 43½

Blue & Gold: 415/773-1188,
www.blueandgoldfleet.com; Red & White:
415/447-0597, www.redandwhite.com

 $18 adults, $14
youths 12–18, $10
children 5–11

 Daily with varying times

5 and up

landmarks such as Coit Tower (*see* listings for many of these sights) and the Transamerica Pyramid. Boats pass by the southern side of Alcatraz, then head west past Presidio National Park and Fort Point on the way toward the Golden Gate Bridge. For many kids, the big thrill of the cruise is passing beneath the bridge, whose towers rise nearly 750 feet in the air. The boats then turn back east, providing good views of the Marin Headlands and the Mediterranean-style village of Sausalito to the north. In the last few minutes you'll circle around Angel Island and then head back south past Alcatraz to the docks.

Even on the bay, which is usually placid compared to the ocean, you might want to take seasickness precautions for your children (check with your pediatrician about appropriate medications). Also remember that it can get very cold and windy on the water, even on a sunny day, so dress in layers.

HEY, KIDS! A lot of people now think that the Transamerica Pyramid, which you can see from the boat, is just about the coolest building in the whole city. But when it was built back in 1972, most San Franciscans seemed to hate it. At 48 stories high, it's not quite the tallest building in the city, but it's probably the most unusual. How many other skyscrapers have you seen with such a pointy top? If you want to get a close-up look at it, have Mom or Dad take you to 600 Montgomery Street, in the Financial District.

BAY MODEL VISITOR CENTER

Everyone knows San Francisco is the City by the Bay, but the size and geography of the bay—as well as other nearby waterways—can be confusing even for longtime residents. This 1½-acre, hydraulic, three-dimensional scale model of the bay, housed inside a onetime shipbuilding facility, helps your family make sense of all that water.

Operated by the U.S. Army Corps of Engineers, the Bay Model looks like a cross between a science experiment and a huge work of modern art. Don't expect bells and whistles, though; this is a scientific facility, built in the 1950s to test possible ways of damming the bay to store fresh water. No dams were built, but the model now enables scientists and engineers to study the bay's water flow and tidal patterns and to measure the effects of both natural phenomena (such as drought and floods) and human activities on local waters. It's all intended to help the corps protect wetlands, control flooding, manage natural disasters, and keep waterways navigable.

KEEP IN MIND Tours of the Bay Model are self-guided, so pick up a map when you enter. If you have a minimum of 10 people in your group, however, you can call in advance to reserve a ranger-led tour. Rangers will gear the presentation toward the ages of the kids and whatever your particular interests are, so round up another like-minded family or two if you can. Audiotape tours are also available, though younger kids might find these boring. Allow about 1½ hours for any tour, all of which are free.

2100 Bridgeway, Sausalito

Free

415/332–3870 recording,
415/332–3871 voice;
www.spn.usace.army.mil/bmvc

Memorial Day–Labor Day, T–F 9–4, Sa–Su
10–5; early Sept–late May, T–Sa 9–4

8 and up

For young visitors (age 9 and up is best), hands-on educational exhibits and videos depict the bay's natural history, wildlife, geology, and fishing industry. You and your children can walk on ramps to get an overview of just how big the bay is. The model comprises nearly 300 12-foot by 12-foot, 5-ton slabs of concrete, representing 343 square miles of bay, river, ocean, and land, all reproduced to scale. The model encompasses the South Bay (down to San Jose), Central Bay (including San Francisco and Oakland), San Pablo Bay (Marin County), the Golden Gate, the narrows of the Carquinez Strait, Suisun Bay (California's largest remaining tidal wetland), and the vast Sacramento Delta's labyrinth of river channels, sloughs, and islands. Though it's worth seeing at any time, the best time to come is when the model is operational and you can actually watch the tides flowing through the bay. So call ahead for schedules, and get ready to discover things you may never have known about San Francisco Bay.

HEY, KIDS! Most of the water in San Francisco Bay comes from rivers. It's called freshwater, which means it isn't salty like ocean water. But the bay water empties into the Pacific at the Golden Gate, where the bridge is, and pretty soon, it's salty, too. Take a taste test sometime!

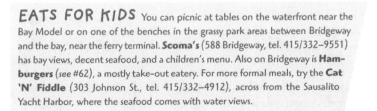

EATS FOR KIDS You can picnic at tables on the waterfront near the Bay Model or on one of the benches in the grassy park areas between Bridgeway and the bay, near the ferry terminal. **Scoma's** (588 Bridgeway, tel. 415/332–9551) has bay views, decent seafood, and a children's menu. Also on Bridgeway is **Hamburgers** (see #62), a mostly take-out eatery. For more formal meals, try the **Cat 'N' Fiddle** (303 Johnson St., tel. 415/332–4912), across from the Sausalito Yacht Harbor, where the seafood comes with water views.

BURLINGAME MUSEUM OF PEZ MEMORABILIA

Housed in a former computer store in the town of Burlingame, just south of San Francisco, this is the world's first and only museum devoted to Pez, the tiny candy that comes in the plastic dispensers with the wacky flip-top heads. The man behind the museum is Gary Doss, who sold computers here for 10 years until the Pez dispensers he started displaying for fun proved more popular than the PCs. Doss has amassed a permanent collection of some 500 dispensers, the largest public display in the world. It's a good bet to delight any child who likes collections or candy—or collecting candy.

Kids can look for dispensers with Disney characters—Mickey Mouse was the first ever, dating from the early 1950s—as well as Santa Claus, the Pink Panther, *Star Wars* characters, Smurfs, Batman, Kermit the Frog and Miss Piggy, the Ninja Turtles, Bugs Bunny, or the all-time best-seller, Winnie-the-Pooh. A display box contains such rarities as Bicentennial Pez, Olympic Pez, Psychedelic Eye Pez (a giant hand with an eyeball in it, from 1968),

HEY, KIDS!

Can you guess where the name "Pez" comes from? It's actually a shortened version of the German word for peppermint: *Pfefferminz*. Pez are made in Austria, where German is the official language. Even if you speak German, "Pez" sure is a lot easier to say.

KEEP IN MIND Yes, the museum's free, but that doesn't mean you won't lighten your wallet here. In the gift shop—bigger than the rest of the museum—your kids (or, more likely, you) can buy plenty of Pez or Pez collectibles, including Pez puzzles, posters, and T-shirts. Chances are you won't leave the museum without a Pezzy purchase—perhaps a Glowing Ghost Pez, Nintendo Pez, or Pez flashlight—but remember that the candy tastes as good from a $2 dispenser as from a $1,000 one. (Your kids might need to be reminded of that, too.)

214 California Dr., Burlingame

 650/347–2301;
www.burlingamepezmuseum.com

 Free

T–F 10–6, Sa 10–5

5 and up

and Arithmetic Pez, which sports a slide rule. The Golden Glow Pez dispenser looks like real gold, but isn't. Pez guns, made from the 1950s until 1982, are another novelty, as are Body Parts Pez, which were made for just three years and are designed to fit over other Pez dispensers. (The skeleton Body Parts is a hit at Halloween.) The museum also shows video clips of Pez appearances in movies—*E.T., Stand By Me, The Client* (which featured an "Elvis Pezley")—and on TV—a Krusty Pez on *The Simpsons,* a Tweety Bird Pez on *Seinfeld*.

Don't get the idea that this is all penny-candy stuff. Lots of people collect dispensers, and Pez conventions are held each year around the country. Doss's most valuable piece is a 1972 "Make-a-Face" dispenser worth about $3,000, taken off the market after a few months because it presented a choking hazard. And if you tossed yours away back then, you're probably choking now.

EATS FOR KIDS **Christie's Restaurant** (245 California Dr., tel. 650/347–9440), which serves breakfast and lunch daily, is right across from the museum. With a counter, a few outdoor tables, and a bustling atmosphere, it dishes up such staples as eggs, burgers, fries, and hot and cold sandwiches. **La Piñata** (1205 Burlingame Ave., tel. 650/375–1070) is a Mexican restaurant within easy walking distance. For good Italian food in nice surroundings, and children's menus to boot, the local branch of **Il Fornaio** (327 Lorton Ave., tel. 650/375–8000) is always reliable.

CABLE CAR MUSEUM

When a cable car comes by—bells clanging, brakes screeching, cables humming—everybody, whether kid or grown-up, turns to watch. Cable cars are the only National Historic Landmarks that *move*. But what is it that makes these Victorian-age conveyances go (without engines!) and keeps them on track—up and down some of the city's steepest hills? You'll find out at the Cable Car Museum.

Of course, first you have to get here, and the only way to go is by cable car. Well, you could drive, but what fun would that be? And parking is nearly impossible to find anyway. Hop on the Powell-Mason Line or the Powell-Hyde Line either downtown or in the Fisherman's Wharf area. Then ask the conductor to call out the Cable Car Museum, situated in the 1907 redbrick cable car barn and powerhouse at the corner of Washington and Mason streets, near Chinatown. The cable car ride costs $2 per person (under 5 free), but with free admission to the museum, you're still ahead of the game.

KEEP IN MIND Cable cars are often crowded, and long lines form at the turn-arounds, where passengers gather to make sure they get seats. But you don't have to board at turnarounds; cars stop every other block or so (look for maroon-and-white signs). If you board en route, approach the car quickly as it pauses, wedge into an available space, and hold on tight. Make sure small children are safely inside, holding on, before the car moves. You can pay on board or buy a ticket at one of the self-service machines at some terminals.

1201 Mason St.Nob Hill, Russian Hill

 Free

Apr–Sept, daily 10–6; Oct–Mar, daily 10–5

415/474–1887;
www.cablecarmuseum.com

3 and up

Once inside on a self-guided tour, you'll learn the ingenious secrets of cable power, developed more than 125 years ago by Andrew Hallidie, an engineer and immigrant from Scotland, who tested the first cable car on nearby Clay Street. It's simple, really: Four sets of cables make a continuous 9½-mph circuit beneath city streets; the cars, which grip the cables, automatically travel along with them. The cable system—on view on the lower level here—is run by huge revolving wheels that pull and steer the cables as they enter and leave the powerhouse. (You can hear the whirring sounds as soon as you come in.) Up on the mezzanine, a museum displays three antique model cable cars, including the first one Hallidie built in 1873. You'll also find plenty of old photographs, a 16-minute film showing how cable cars operate, and a museum shop. After a visit here, your kids will probably clamor for another cable car ride right away.

EATS FOR KIDS
The **Cable Car Diner** (Clay and Powell Sts., tel. 415/986-3192) has an eclectic menu ranging from breakfasts and burgers to Chinese and Mexican dishes. The **Pot Sticker** (150 Waverly Pl., tel. 415/397–9985) has good, inexpensive Chinese food, such as panfried dumplings filled with meat or vegetables.

HEY, KIDS! When you take a cable car ride, be sure to keep an eye on the gripman and brakeman in action. The gripman works the lever that grips the cable beneath the street, making the car go forward. If he lets go, the car stops—with the help of the brakeman, who works the brakes. On steep hills and around curves, especially, the two men have to rely on teamwork, timing, and muscle. Sometimes watching them work is more fun than watching the scenery.

CALIFORNIA ACADEMY OF SCIENCES

57

This huge complex in the heart of Golden Gate Park is actually three family attractions in one—a natural history museum, aquarium, and planetarium providing windows into the earth, ocean, and space.

Start with the Natural History Museum, one of the world's 10 largest. Your kids will come face to face (or face to ankle) with a skeleton of a Tyrannosaurus rex and other dinosaur fossils. At the Earthquake! exhibit, you can experience simulated quakes, complete with special effects, so Californians can get psyched for the Big One and out-of-staters can see what the fuss is about. At the Africa Experience, your kids can touch an elephant skin and compare their legs to a giraffe's. Kids 5 and under can head to the Africa Playspace, where they can try on costumes and watch puppet shows.

At the Steinhart Aquarium, included in museum admission, kids can eyeball thousands of fresh- and saltwater fish and other aquatic creatures. Whether it's piranhas, manatees,

HEY, KIDS!
When you're at the Fish Roundabout, try to follow one fish as it swims all the way around the circle. Not easy, is it? The Roundabout is 204 feet around, with 36 windows. Does your fish ever stop or change direction? It's fun to watch, but you might get dizzy.

KEEP IN MIND You can save money on admission here by riding public transit to Golden Gate Park; show a valid ticket, transfer, or monthly pass and get $2.50 off general admission to the museum—enough savings to attend a planetarium show for "free." (The Muni No. 44 O'Shaughnessy bus goes directly to the front entrance.) The museum is free to all on the first Wednesday of each month, and it also has a variety of "neighborhood free days" each fall, for San Francisco residents only; call 415/750–7144 for more information.

55 Concourse Dr., near 8th Ave. and Fulton St., Golden Gate Park

 $8.50 adults, $5.50 youths 12–17 and students, $2 children 4–11; planetarium $2.50 adults, $1.25 children 6–17; 1st W of mth free

 Memorial Day–Labor Day, daily 9–6; early Sept–late May, daily 10–5

415/750–7145 recording, 415/ 221–5100 voice, 415/750–7127 planetarium; www.calacademy.org

 2 and up; planetarium 6 and up

jellyfish, sea horses, seals, dolphins, electric fish, or alligators lying still as logs, you can find them in some 165 tanks approximating natural habitats. In the 600,000-gallon living tropical reef, you'll see reef sharks and brilliantly colored fish swimming around equally beautiful coral. Young children, especially, like to get their hands wet at the Touch Tidepool, where they can pick up sea stars, anemones, and slimy sea cucumbers. Be sure to visit the aquarium's cute black-footed penguins at feeding time: 11:30 and 4. At the Fish Roundabout, where leopard sharks, sea bass, tuna, and pompano swim in a 100,000-gallon circular tank, you can watch the feeding frenzy daily at 1:30.

The Morrison Planetarium's 40-minute star shows, which cost extra, reveal the night sky through the ages under a 55-foot dome. Music and special effects take you whirling through galaxies and into black holes; it's exciting, but potentially frightening for preschoolers. You'll see the sky as you've never seen it from the city, but then, everything in this complex seems to be like entering another world.

EATS FOR KIDS The museum's **cafeteria** is open until an hour before closing. **The Canvas** (1200 9th Ave., tel. 415/504–0060) is a light, airy, casual café with a park view; *panini* (Italian-style) sandwiches, focaccia pizzas, and yummy baked goods are among the offerings. **Park Chow** (1240 9th Ave., tel. 415/665–9912) is a bustling place with both indoor and out-door tables and an eclectic menu ranging from spaghetti and little pizzas to Asian-style noodles. This one's best suited for kids 10 and up, or, if younger, with sophisticated tastes.

CALIFORNIA PALACE OF THE LEGION OF HONOR

One of the city's top fine-arts museums, the California Palace of the Legion of Honor is a showcase for European paintings, sculpture, tapestries, and furniture dating from medieval times. Works by the French Impressionists and the sculptor Auguste Rodin are highlights. Equally stunning is the gleaming palace-like structure itself, which was designed in 1924 in the style of the 18th-century Palais de Legion d'Honneur in Paris and intended as a memorial to California's World War I dead. Renovated in the 1990s, with a pyramidal glass skylight illuminating the new lower-level galleries, the museum occupies a splendid location in Lincoln Park, in the Richmond District. Rodin's famous sculpture *The Thinker*, made from an 1880 cast, sits just outside the front entrance.

Depending on the ages of your children, allow about an hour or two for a typical visit. Stick to the basics. Many school-age kids enjoy paintings by French Impressionists, and the museum has one of Monet's famous *Water Lilies*. Be sure to take them to the two Rodin galleries, too, which contain about 70 works by the French sculptor (see if they can spot

HEY, KIDS! Think art museums are boring? The story behind this one isn't. It all started because of a rivalry between two wealthy San Francisco families. Millionaire Adolph Spreckels and his wife, Alma, financed the palace, at least partly, to outdo the de Youngs, who had built a museum in Golden Gate Park. Adolph even shot and wounded M.H. de Young, publisher of the *San Francisco Chronicle*, which had printed stories about him that he didn't like. How's that for a real soap opera?

100 34th Ave., Lincoln Park (enter park at Clement St. and 34th Ave.)

415/863-3330; www.thinker.org/legion

 $8 adults, $5 youths 12–17; $2 off with Muni transfer; T free

T–Su 9:30–5

6 and up

the one called *Man With a Broken Nose*). And if your kids haven't been exposed to much European art, they can see their first examples of Peter Paul Rubens and Rembrandt here.

On most Saturday afternoons at 2, you can take part in one of the special 1½-hour, drop-in programs the museum offers for kids and their parents. Kids ages 7–12 can attend Doing and Viewing Art, which includes gallery tours and art classes. Younger art aficionados (ages 3½–6) get their own chance to see and try their hands at art in Big Kids, Little Kids (parental accompaniment required for this one). The programs are free with paid museum admission, but call ahead (tel. 415/750-3658) to make sure they are offered the day you come. They're a great way to introduce even preschoolers to the world of art, and your kids might just surprise you with their enthusiasm.

KEEP IN MIND Lincoln Park has 270 acres of greenery. At its eastern end, 200-foot-high cliffs offer dramatic views of the Golden Gate Bridge, and hiking trails lead off along the headlands. The public Lincoln Park Golf Course (tel. 415/221–9911) is reasonably priced for its exceptional setting.

EATS FOR KIDS The museum's attractive **Legion of Honor Cafe** (tel. 415/221–2233) offers Pacific views along with good sandwiches and salads. Weekend lunch lines can get brutal, though, so it's often quicker (and cheaper) to eat elsewhere. Local favorite **Bill's Place** (2315 Clement St., tel. 415/221–5262) is known for its juicy burgers and patio dining. Families flock to the outstanding dim sum and other Chinese food at **Ton Kiang** (5821 Geary Blvd., tel. 415/387–8273), so get here early, especially on weekends.

CALIFORNIA STATE RAILROAD MUSEUM

55

The city of Sacramento (about 90 miles east of San Francisco via I–80) gave birth to the idea for the first transcontinental railroad. So it's a fitting setting for this outstanding facility, the largest interpretive railroad museum in North America. In fact, the 19th century is very much alive at the museum, part of Old Sacramento State Historic Park—a 28-acre restored Gold Rush–era district with Victorian buildings, wooden boardwalks, gas lamps, and cobbled streets—lying along the Sacramento River. A host of beautifully restored historic train cars, including five of the still-existing 30 full-size steam locomotives built in the United States before 1880, share the spotlight. Films, slide shows, and exhibits recount the role the trains played in history. Volunteers, many of them ex-railway workers, are on hand to answer questions.

The oldest locomotive in the collection, the 1863 Southern Pacific *No. 1 C.P. Huntington*, was used in building the transcontinental railroad. But that one is dwarfed by an enormous 1944 Southern Pacific steam locomotive, one of the largest ever. It's 125

EATS FOR KIDS For 1870s-era atmosphere and contemporary food, head for the **Silver Palace Restaurant** (920 Front St., tel. 916/448–0151), in the Central Pacific Railroad Passenger Station. Another colorful choice nearby, the **Pilothouse Restaurant** (1000 Front St., tel. 916/441–4440), aboard a vintage paddle wheeler, serves seafood.

HEY, KIDS! Just down from the museum is a hardware store where several rich businessmen met to plan the first transcontinental railroad. One railroad company, Central Pacific, began building tracks in 1863 in Sacramento; the other, Union Pacific, began in Nebraska. When they met in the middle, at Promontory, Utah, in 1869, they drove a golden spike into the ground to mark the occasion. After that, people and goods could cross the country much more easily. The railroad played a huge role in settling the West and taming the frontier.

2nd and I Sts., Sacramento

 916/445-6645;
www.californiastaterailroadmuseum.org

 $3 ages 17 and up

 Daily 10–5

6 and up

feet long and weighs more than a million pounds. Your kids can walk through the 1929 Canadian National Railways sleeper the *St. Hyacinthe,* in which special light, sound, and rocking-motion effects create the illusion of clattering down the rails during the night. Another walk-through exhibit, the Dinner in the Diner, features a luxury passenger-train dining car set with china service. A 1937 menu shows that full meals (salmon, swordfish, roast beef) cost less than $1 and the kids' menu was 50¢.

Upstairs, you'll find exhibits on classic model trains, including ones used in the movies *E.T.* and *Throw Momma From the Train.* Tickets to the museum also include admission to the nearby reconstructed Central Pacific Passenger Station (930 Front St.), a circa-1870 station with separate waiting rooms for ladies and children and a refreshment stand selling sarsaparilla. All aboard!

KEEP IN MIND You could easily spend the rest of a day exploring Old Sacramento State Historic Park (tel. 916/442–7644). Your family can take a horse-drawn carriage ride or paddle-wheeler cruise along the river, or, on weekends April–September, ride along the river on a steam train: the Sacramento Southern Railroad ($6 ages 13 and up, $3 children 6–12). There's also an old schoolhouse to tour, a vintage theater, a Wells Fargo museum, and the Discovery Museum (101 L St., tel. 916/264–7057), a hands-on science and history facility.

CARTOON ART MUSEUM

Old toons never die. They just go to the Cartoon Art Museum. This is the place where Bill Watterson's classic comic duo, Calvin and Hobbes, live on. So do old-timers Krazy Kat and the Green Lantern. You'll also find the familiar figures of Snoopy, Charlie Brown, Batman, Bugs Bunny, and Dennis the Menace. Here, cartoons are treated with all the reverence usually accorded other types of art. Founded in 1984, it's the only museum on the West Coast that's dedicated to preserving, collecting, and exhibiting original cartoon art in all its forms.

In late 2001, the museum moved into a new, larger location down the street from its aging galleries in the South of Market area, near Yerba Buena Gardens (*see* #1). The new location contains five spacious exhibit areas as well as an expanded bookstore.

The museum's 12,000-piece permanent collection displays works from 1730 (a political cartoon by William Hogarth, an English artist considered the father of modern caricature) to 1895 (the Yellow Kid, the first successful newspaper comic strip character) to modern day

HEY, KIDS! At the museum, you'll see several drawings used to make Bugs Bunny and other animated cartoons. But did you know that artists have to make 24 separate drawings to produce just one second of running film? That's 1,440 different drawings for each minute— and 86,400 for each hour! Each drawing is done on a clear plastic "cel," which is then photographed over a painted background to make Bugs, Porky Pig, and Elmer Fudd come alive in the finished film.

 655 Mission St.

 $5 adults, $3 students, $2 children 6–12; classes $35

W–F 11–5, Sa 10–5, Su 1–5

5 and up

415/227–8666; www.cartoonart.org

("Peanuts," "Doonesbury," "Zippy the Pinhead" strips). Included in the collection, besides comic strips, are editorial cartoons, comic books (including underground and avant-garde), magazines, advertisements, newspapers, sculptures, and animation drawings. Among the latter, look for animation cels from Bugs Bunny cartoons, Pink Panther productions, and Peanuts TV shows as well as Disney studio drawings from such films as *Pinocchio, Fantasia, Snow White, Peter Pan,* and *101 Dalmatians.* Your kids may also enjoy discovering old-time comic strip artists like Jimmy Hatlo ("They'll Do It Every Time") and Harold Foster ("Prince Valiant").

At the museum's Children's Gallery, kids ages 8–14 can take cartooning classes. Given by a professional cartoonist, they teach kids how to draw some of their favorite cartoon characters as well as how to create their own strips. Classes last 2½ hours and cost $35, with materials included; call the museum for times. Maybe someday your own child's work will adorn these same walls.

KEEP IN MIND
Some cartoons on display (especially in special exhibitions) may be R- or X-rated. If this is a concern, you may want to do a little advance scouting or call the museum first before bringing your kids and being unpleasantly surprised.

EATS FOR KIDS Just up the street, conveniently tucked alongside the nearest public parking garage, a branch of **Mels Drive-In** (801 Mission St., tel. 415/227–4477) serves up big, juicy burgers and tasty fountain drinks with a colorful '50s-diner theme. Kids' meals are served in cardboard classic cars. For other family-friendly spots in the immediate area, ranging from casual cafés to bustling ethnic eateries (Italian, Mexican, Asian), see the San Francisco Museum of Modern Art and Yerba Buena Gardens.

CHABOT SPACE AND SCIENCE CENTER

In mid-2000, the Chabot Space and Science Center, an observatory since 1883, moved from its previous home in the Oakland Hills into a new, $70 million, state-of-the-art facility a few miles away in Joaquin Miller Park, also in the Oakland Hills. At its new, higher elevation (1,540 feet), the observatory provides access to the country's largest telescope that's regularly open to the public—a 36-inch reflector. Historic 8-inch and 20-inch refractors are still on hand, too.

But kids and parents have gotten much more than a new observatory. Among the new attractions at the facility's innovative space center is a 275-seat planetarium, one of the most advanced in the world, presenting dazzling star shows daily. And the large-screen, 225-seat domed Science Theater features 30-minute films such as *To Be an Astronaut* and *Mysteries of Egypt*. The circular screen and sound virtually surround you.

GETTING THERE Take I–580 to Highway 13 south. Exit at Joaquin Miller/Lincoln Avenue, and go east on Joaquin Miller. Turn left onto Skyline Boulevard. After 1.3 miles, turn right into the space center. Alternatively, take the No. 53 AC Transit bus from the Fruitvale BART station.

KEEP IN MIND You can easily run up a big tab here. If you add a planetarium show to regular admission, it's $14.75 for an adult and $11 for a child; if you add the science theater as well, it's $19.75 and $15.50. (There is a $1 discount for students with ID.) Parking is $4, and you may drop a few bucks in the well-stocked science store as well. If you go for the whole enchilada, plan to make a day of it to get your money's worth.

10902 Skyline Blvd., Oakland

 510/530-3480;
www.chabotspace.org

 $8 ages 13 and up, $5.50 children 4–12; planetarium and theater extra

 T–Sa 10–5, Su 12–5; planetarium and observatory additional hrs

 6 and up

Meanwhile, three exhibition halls house a variety of permanent and temporary, hands-on exhibits focusing on astronomy and the interrelationships of all sciences and technology. Our Place in the Universe takes you on a short walk from the Oakland Hills into the outer solar system and then deep into distant galaxies. More fun for kids, though, are the changing, hands-on exhibits upstairs. For example, in Planetary Landscapes, kids got to "rearrange" the earth's landscape, showing how nothing ever stays the same. Also here are the Challenger Learning Center, which transforms you into a scientist, engineer, or researcher on a simulated space mission, complete with mission control and spacecraft; the Discovery Lab, with science-related art projects; and a computer lab. Outdoors, the EnviroGarden is a 6-acre environmental education area with a pond, stream, and nature trail. Customized backpacks with magnifiers, field microscopes, collecting bottles, and field guides are available for use on walks with naturalists.

EATS FOR KIDS The space center's ultra-casual, self-serve **Celestial Café** offers sandwiches (roast beef, turkey, PB&J) as well as fresh fruit and drinks. There are both indoor and outdoor tables, the latter on a terrace with nice views looking down over Oakland. You can also bring your own food to eat here. Joaquin Miller Park has plenty of picnic space, and there's a branch of **Round Table Pizza** (2854 Mountain Blvd., tel. 510/482–1111) down the hill a bit from the space center. For restaurants in Oakland's Lake Merritt area (a fair distance away), see #52.

CHILDREN'S FAIRYLAND

52

This 10-acre storybook theme park, the first of its kind in the country, has another possible claim to fame: Walt Disney himself visited here a few years before opening Disneyland in 1955, and it may have helped inspire the idea for the Magic Kingdom. One thing's certain: Children's Fairyland has enchanted local children for more than a half century. You won't find any teens zooming by on daredevil rides or any high-tech gadgets catering to the over-10 set here. At this clean, low-key theme park, the stage is set entirely for young kids.

A Magic Key, purchased for a one-time fee, unlocks "talking storybooks," bringing more than 30 colorful nursery rhyme and fairy-tale sets to life. Your children can gaze through the window of Geppetto's workshop, pass through Alice in Wonderland's tunnel, enter the mouth of Willie the Whale, visit Peter Rabbit's Village, and view the Three Billy Goats Gruff—complete with live goats. Play Island, based on the tale of the Swiss Family Robinson, is like a multilevel tree house complete with bridges, tropical-style huts, and sound effects.

KEEP IN MIND After visiting Children's Fairyland, you can explore other parts of 120-acre Lakeside Park, on pretty Lake Merritt. A natural saltwater lake—a rare phenomenon in the middle of a city—Lake Merritt was the country's first state game refuge, and there's still a waterfowl refuge here. Playgrounds, gardens, picnic spots, a natural science center, a bandstand, and waterfowl-feeding areas await at various points around the park. You can take a stroll or even a boat ride around the lake or rent rowboats, canoes, paddleboats, or small sailboats from the Lake Merritt Boating Center (tel. 510/444–3807).

699 Bellevue Ave., at Grand Ave., Lakeside Park, Oakland

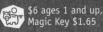 $6 ages 1 and up, Magic Key $1.65

Apr–mid-June and Sept, W–Su 10–4; mid-June–Aug, M–F 10–4:30, Sa–Su 10–5; Oct–Mar, F–Su 10–4

1–9

510/238–6876 recording, 510/452–2259 voice; www.fairyland.org

Puppet shows, storytelling, and a little animal corral with donkeys, rabbits, ponies, and sheep—kids can pet them from 1 to 2 on weekends—provide more entertainment. So do a few gentle mini-rides—a carousel, a Ferris wheel, a boat ride, a trolley, and a train—all of which are included in the unlimited-ride admission price.

Children's Fairyland has recently added a spiffy new entrance complete with a topiary Chinese dragon, as well as a tree-shaded village square, an Arabian Nights–themed gift shop, and a café. The park hosts a number of special events throughout the year, including a spring maypole dance, a summer Mad Hatter's Tea Party, and a Halloween Jack-O-Lantern Jamboree, when sets and rides get taken over by ghosts, pirates, and other scary things. There are also performing arts summer camps for kids 5–11, roles for kids 8–10 in Fairyland plays (audition required), and overnight family campouts in summer. With all this, who needs Disneyland?

HEY, KIDS! Children's Fairyland has been giving Red Riding Hood puppet shows since way back in 1968. Did you know that the story first came from Germany? The Brothers Grimm included it in their book of fairy tales, but there's nothing "grim" about the fun way they tell it here.

EATS FOR KIDS Fairyland's new **Johnny Appleseed Café** serves hot dogs, burgers, fruit, and drinks in a casual garden setting, and the park has picnic areas, too. You can also bring your own food to picnic along the banks of Lake Merritt, where plenty of grass and shade trees invite spreading out a blanket. **Zza's Trattoria** (552 Grand Ave., tel. 510/839–9124) is an informal, child-friendly Italian restaurant near the lake. **Zachary's Chicago Pizza** (5801 College Ave., tel. 510/655–6385) has some of the area's best deep-dish pies.

CHINA BEACH

Pocket-size China Beach isn't a snap to find, but for those who seek it out, a reward awaits: It's one of the few beaches in San Francisco where it's generally gentle and safe enough to swim. Named for a group of poor Chinese fishermen who lived beside the beach during the Gold Rush era and now tucked below the palatial homes of the tony Seacliff area in the Richmond District, China Beach is a 600-foot sandy strip that's shielded by cliffs on either side. Its sheltered location heads off the treacherous waves that batter other, better-known city beaches, such as Ocean Beach (*see* #20), and make swimming at those beaches so risky. It's also off the beaten track, so it seldom gets too crowded.

Not that China Beach is an entirely pleasant place to take a dip. The water tends to be pretty chilly, hovering around the 60s in summer, and, like all San Francisco beaches, it can get socked in by summer fog. But if you can get past the teeth-chattering, it's a nice

HEY, KIDS!
Acclaimed actor Robin Williams lives with his family in a mansion just above China Beach. You might see him out running nearby. Kids gather from all over at Halloween to trick-or-treat at his house, hoping to catch a glimpse of Robin himself.

EATS FOR KIDS There are no restaurants right next to China Beach, so the handiest thing to do is pack a picnic lunch or snacks or use the beach's barbecue facilities. Friendly **Thanh Thanh Café** (2205 Clement St., tel. 415/387–1759) serves up inexpensive, casual breakfasts and lunches; choose between Vietnamese sandwiches and noodle dishes or American-style eggs, burgers, and hot dogs. For details on other Richmond District restaurants—**Bill's Place** (hamburgers) and **Ton Kiang** (Chinese food)—see the California Palace of the Legion of Honor.

spot to bring swimming-age kids and let them wade off into the water without undue fears (there are no longer lifeguards here, however, so keep a close watch). Though small compared to other beaches, China Beach still has room to toss a Frisbee around, and you'll be treated to views of the Golden Gate and the Marin Headlands that match the million-dollar price tags of the homes perched above. You might even spot a marine mammal or two—perhaps a sea lion or a daredevil surfer (the human variety).

The facilities are good here, too (it's run by the National Park Service). You'll find free changing rooms, showers, rest rooms, barbecue pits, picnic tables, and—if lying on sand isn't your thing—an enclosed sundeck for stretching out on your beach towel. Those with tots can push strollers all the way to the beach; look for the ramp on the left side. Small though it is, China Beach manages to pack a lot in.

GETTING THERE To reach the somewhat-elusive China Beach, take El Camino del Mar to the area around Seacliff Avenue and 26th Avenue. Park in the small lot (which fills up early on weekends) or on the street, and walk down the hill. The No. 1 California Muni bus stops a few blocks away. If you pull out a map and see the name James D. Phelan Beach in this location, don't be confused; that's just an older name for China Beach.

CHINATOWN

Chinatown can be magical for kids: Neon signs, pagoda roofs, dragon-entwined lampposts, and shops packed with strange-looking herbs all add to its exotic allure. One of the largest Chinese communities outside Asia, it's a tightly packed, colorful 24-block jumble of restaurants, teahouses, temples, souvenir shops, and markets.

The only way to see the area is on foot. Start at the green-tiled, dragon-topped Chinatown Gate (Bush St. and Grant Ave.). It's much like entering a city within a city. Walk north up Grant Avenue—Chinatown's main thoroughfare—lined with bazaars, restaurants, and curio shops. Some items, often piled high in baskets on the sidewalk, are quite inexpensive. But don't limit yourself to Grant. To the west, Stockton Street (where Chinese shop for produce and fresh fish) has a more authentic feel, as do many small alleyways nearby. The Chinese Six Companies Building (843 Stockton St.), with curved roof tiles and pagoda top, should catch your kids' eyes. Along narrow side streets like Hang Ah, Spofford Lane, and Ross Alley, you can hear the click of mah-jongg tiles, the whir of sewing machines, and the clinking

KEEP IN MIND One of the most colorful times to visit Chinatown is during the Chinese New Year, generally in late February or early March. The Chinese New Year Parade (tel. 415/391–9680), held on a Saturday evening, is one of few remaining illuminated night parades. Some 500,000 spectators pack Chinatown and the Financial District to watch marching bands, floats, lion dancers, martial artists, acrobats, towering Chinese deities, and Gum Lum, a 200-foot-long golden dragon with 35 dancers inside. Firecrackers may frighten young children, however. The Chinatown Street Fair, the same weekend, features kite making, lion dancing, and calligraphy.

Bounded by Columbus Ave. and Bush, Kearny, Vallejo, and Powell Sts.

 Free

Daily 24 hrs

415/982-6306; www.sfchinatown.com

 5 and up

of teacups. At the Golden Gate Fortune Cookie Factory (56 Ross Alley, tel. 415/781-3956), your kids can discover how fortunes get inside.

The Tien Hou Temple (125 Waverly Pl.) is the oldest Buddhist temple in the United States; climb to the third floor, where the air is redolent of incense and the decor features red-and-gold lanterns and carved wooden deities. The Chinese Culture Center, in the Holiday Inn (750 Kearny St., tel. 415/986-1822), presents small exhibits; the most fun for kids may be walking over Kearny via the footbridge. The best museum is the Chinese Historical Society of America (965 Clay St., tel. 415/391-1188), which documents the history of Chinese immigrants and their descendants. At Portsmouth Square, site of an early settlement, elders greet the morning with tai chi exercises. Men then play cards and a Chinese version of chess, while grandmothers watch children on the playground. It's all part of life, Chinese-American style.

HEY, KIDS! San Francisco has one of the largest Chinese populations in the world outside Asia. Chinese first came here during the Gold Rush, in 1848, settling down in Chinatown's Portsmouth Square. Today, about one in every five San Franciscans is of Chinese descent, and most live outside Chinatown.

EATS FOR KIDS For a snack, get almond cookies, moon cakes, or steamed pork buns at one of the many Chinese bakeries, or buy fortune cookies. For lunch, try dim sum (filled dumplings and other small dishes, usually chosen from carts wheeled from table to table). The huge **New Asia** (772 Pacific Ave., tel. 415/391-6666) and **Pearl City** (641 Jackson St., tel. 415/398-8383) are both good choices. **Great Eastern** (649 Jackson St., tel. 415/986-2500) has excellent fresh seafood, exemplified by their fish tanks. For information on the **Pot Sticker**, see #58.

CLIFF HOUSE

istoric Cliff House, perched above Ocean Beach and the Pacific at San Francisco's westernmost tip, has some of the city's best views of land and sea, making it a standard tour bus stop. Built in 1909, it's the third Cliff House on this site since 1863; the other two burned down. Today it houses popular restaurants, a bar, and an adjacent National Park Service visitor center, whose historical and natural history displays include fascinating old photos of both previous Cliff House incarnations—one of which was of gingerbread Victorian design and rose eight stories high.

Surprising treasures await kids who couldn't care less about the views, history, or restaurants. Near the visitor center is the Musée Mécanique (tel. 415/386–1170), a quirky penny arcade—quarters are today's currency—with mechanical games old and new. It brims with player pianos, pinball machines, nickelodeons, and miscellaneous oddities such as a miniature amusement park made of toothpicks by San Quentin Prison inmates. Just around the corner is an unusual camera obscura, a replica of an invention by Leonardo da Vinci.

KEEP IN MIND Just across the Great Highway (atop the cliffs) from the Cliff House lies often overlooked Sutro Heights Park, where old-time millionaire Adolph Sutro's mansion once stood. The park has picnic tables, shade trees, paths, gardens, and more great ocean views.

HEY, KIDS! Imagine the Sutro Baths as they once looked. The seven saltwater pools—filled with 1,685,000 gallons of water that was kept at different temperatures for different pools—used to draw up to 20,000 swimmers a day. There were slides, trapezes, springboards, and a high dive, as well as stage shows, restaurants, and artworks on display. In a lot of ways, it was like the country's first water park. Later, before they burned down in 1966, the baths became an ice rink. Now it looks like the ruins of an ancient civilization.

Its lens displays images from outside on a matte-finish dish inside. You might see people on the beach below, or, on a clear day, the Farallon Islands, 27 miles offshore.

From the overlook near the camera obscura, your children can watch for sea lions basking and barking on the offshore Seal Rocks. Traditionally, these huge pinnipeds come here October–June, but nowadays most have deserted the area for Pier 39 (*see* #18). Just north of Seal Rocks, you can gaze down at the ruins of the Sutro Baths, which, from 1896 until they burned down 70 years later, formed the world's largest indoor swimming complex. Today you can make your way down a relatively steep path to walk along the foundations. But watch young kids carefully, and avoid the parts near the water.

In 2002 and 2003, the Cliff House will undergo renovations but will remain open. So there's no reason to stay away and every reason to keep returning.

EATS FOR KIDS You can picnic at Sutro Heights Park or Ocean Beach. **Cliff House** (tel. 415/386–3330) is geared to tourists, but it's hard to top the views. Dining is either upstairs (best for breakfasts and light lunches) or in the downstairs dining room, specializing in seafood. Kids can order small portions. There's also a deli and **Pronto Pup,** a hot dog stand. **Louis'** (902 Point Lobos Ave., tel. 415/387–6330), overlooking the Pacific and the Sutro Baths, serves diner food to happy locals at non-tourist prices.

COIT TOWER AND TELEGRAPH HILL

Folklore has it that 210-foot Coit Tower, which crowns the crest of 248-foot Telegraph Hill, was built to resemble the end of a fire hose. This may be a myth, but there's some logic to it: The stone-white concrete tower was intended as a monument to the city's volunteer firefighters. (Lillie Hitchcock Coit, who bequeathed the funds that paid for it, was a wealthy and eccentric heiress with a passion for fire engines—and firemen.) Since 1933, when it was completed, the tower has become one of San Francisco's most distinctive landmarks, with only the Golden Gate Bridge and perhaps the Transamerica Pyramid more recognized as symbols of the city.

Coit Tower also offers some of San Francisco's best views—an exciting panorama of hills, islands, bridges, and the bay spreading out below. The 360° vista from the top of the tower's Observation Gallery, reached by elevator, is the most encompassing; however, if you come in the evening after the Observation Gallery has closed—when the tower is lit up like a beacon—or you don't want to ride to the top, you can simply enjoy the free views outside.

GETTING THERE The easiest way to walk to the tower is via Lombard Street (not the famous crooked part) and up a flight of steps. It's still steep, though. If you drive up, you may be in for a headache. Parking is tight and the lot at the top is often filled, which can result in a long, frustrating traffic tie-up with no way to turn back. A good alternative is the No. 39 Coit bus, which leaves from the corner of Union Street and Columbus Avenue, at Washington Square.

Telegraph Hill Blvd. at
Greenwich or Lombard Sts.

415/362-0808

 Observation Gallery
$3.75 ages 13 and up,
$1.50 children 6–12

 Observation Gallery daily 10–6:30

 6 and up

Inside the tower, on the ground floor, are murals that were painted by 25 artists as a public works project during the Depression; they depict California's working people in a socialist-realist style pioneered by Mexican artist Diego Rivera.

If your kids are good walkers—don't try this with a stroller—you can opt for either of two easy-to-overlook routes to go back down the hill. Both the Filbert Steps and Greenwich Steps, steep staircase walks that parallel each other as they lead down toward the bay from the east side of Telegraph Hill, are flanked by terraced gardens and secluded homes. While you're taking in more great views of the bay on the way down, your kids can play explorer—as long as they stay out of the residents' backyards. You'll have intriguing glimpses into a hidden corner of the city. But unless your last name is Masochist, get *up* Telegraph Hill by a more conventional route.

HEY, KIDS! Telegraph Hill was once known as Signal Hill for the semaphore (or flag) placed atop it in 1850, which let local merchants know that ships were arriving. But when the West Coast's first telegraph station was built here in 1853, its name changed to—well, guess what?

EATS FOR KIDS Pick up picnic supplies at **Molinari's** (373 Columbus Ave., tel. 415/421–2337), a colorful Italian deli in North Beach, and then have a feast in Washington Square Park. **Tommaso's** (1042 Kearny St., tel. 415/398–9696) crisp, thin-crust pizzas may be San Francisco's all-time favorite. You may have to wait for a table, so come early (dinner only; no reservations). **Mo's Gourmet Hamburgers** (1322 Grant Ave., tel. 415/788–3779), in North Beach, serves up, you guessed it, a variety of big, juicy burgers in casual surroundings.

COYOTE POINT PARK AND MUSEUM

Coyote Point Park, a bay-side recreational area of greenery and sand about 2 miles south of San Francisco International Airport, can easily be an all-day destination. You'll find tree-shaded walking trails with bay overlooks, bike paths, picnic areas, playfields and playgrounds, a fishing jetty, a marina, a summer swimming beach, a saltwater marsh, an adjacent public golf course, and a modern, highly regarded nature museum.

The Coyote Point Museum for Environmental Education makes Coyote Point an all-weather destination, too. Even on a nice day, be sure to leave some time for it. Here, your kids can see live animals native to the Bay Area displayed in realistic habitats. Look for river otters, burrowing owls, porcupines, badgers, skunks, birds of prey, toads, snakes, lizards, bobcats—even lowly banana slugs. A walk-through outdoor aviary provides close-up looks at a variety of birds.

Along with lots of light and space and fun-to-follow wooden ramps connecting the

KEEP IN MIND On a sunny weekend day, it's wise to arrive early to beat the crowds. About the only thing lacking at Coyote Point, besides roller coasters and pizza stands, is enough parking to accommodate all the family cars pouring in for a day's fun in the sunshine.

HEY, KIDS! Let's talk banana slugs, like those you might see at the museum. They're the slimy yellow creatures that you often spot crawling along the trails in cool redwood forests, and they're only found along the West Coast. Some kids like to step on them, but we know you'd never do that. For one thing, they help redwood trees grow. The University of California at Santa Cruz, south of here along the coast, even named the banana slug its official mascot. Go Slugs!

Park, bay side of U.S. 101, San Mateo; museum, 1651 Coyote Point Dr., San Mateo

 Park $4 per car. Museum $3 adults, $2 youths 13–17, $1 children 4–12; 1st W of mth free

 Park daily sunrise–sunset; museum T–Sa 10–5, Su 12–5

650/573–2592 park, 650/342–7755 museum; www.coyoteptmuseum.org

 3 and up

displays, the museum contains computer games, interactive exhibits, and an Environmental Hall that leads you through the Bay Area's major ecosystems: redwood forest, chaparral, grassland, oak woodland, and coastal. It's like taking a walk from the Santa Cruz Mountains to the Pacific Ocean (but a lot easier on your feet). Though the museum is especially well suited to school-age kids, any child 3 or older can enjoy the displays. A well-stocked nature store is attached.

Pick up a flyer on current museum events for families, which might include periodic Family Activity Days and occasional Wild Wednesdays, when the museum stays open late to better showcase nocturnal animals. Also check for temporary exhibitions, which often include wild animals and hands-on displays and may warrant a visit all by themselves. In summer, five-day Summer Discovery Camps let kids 7–10 meet animals, go tide-pooling at an ocean beach, and go hiking, too. Then next time the whole family comes, your former camper can play tour guide.

EATS FOR KIDS The park contains several picnic areas near the water; if you have a large group, you can call to reserve tables. In nearby Burlingame, the **Copenhagen Bakery** (1216 Burlingame Ave., tel. 650/344–4937) has sandwiches you can take out. For other restaurants in Burlingame, see #59. Come to think of it, why not combine a trip to Coyote Point with a stop at the Pez museum and snack on some candies along the way?

THE EMBARCADERO

If San Francisco's 1989 earthquake had one positive effect, it was the subsequent tearing down of the quake-damaged Embarcadero Freeway. For decades, that elevated river of concrete had obscured bay views and blocked the sunlight along this 3-mile, bay-side route. Now the area has blossomed into a promenade for walkers, runners, rollerbladers, renegade skateboarders, sun worshipers, restaurant goers, and those who simply wish to gaze out at the endless procession of sailboats, tugboats, barges, freighters, ferries, cruise ships— and the occasional submarine—on their way from port to port or out to sea.

The centerpiece of the Embarcadero, at the foot of Market Street, is the historic, century-old Ferry Building. Its 230-foot clock tower, once the tallest structure west of the Mississippi, remains a distinctive city landmark. Until 1958, 170 ferries disembarked here daily, and, even as the building undergoes long-term renovation, it remains a departure point for ferries to the East and North bays. Across from the Ferry Building is Justin Herman Plaza, site of the 30-foot-wide Vallaincourt Fountain and, in winter, an outdoor ice rink. Next to the

EATS FOR KIDS At **Town's End Restaurant and Bakery** (2 Townsend St., tel. 415/512–0749), the specialties are great breakfasts and delicious baked goods. A branch of **Boudin Sourdough Bakery & Cafe** (4 Embarcadero Center, tel. 415/362–3330) has a great location on Justin Herman Plaza. You can sit at an outdoor table and eat clam chowder in a bread bowl. At the upscale **Fog City Diner** (1300 Battery St., at the Embarcadero, tel. 415/982–2000), families can share a variety of "small plates" or opt for burgers and shakes.

plaza begin the five skyscrapers of the Embarcadero Center (tel. 800/733-6318), which house shops, restaurants, and a 41st-floor indoor-outdoor observation area called SkyDeck, atop One Embarcadero Center (the farthest tower from the bay).

The Embarcadero is lined with piers, most now put to purposes other than shipping. South of the Ferry Building, all piers are even numbered; to the north, they're odd numbered. Pier 7, just north of the Ferry Building, has been converted into a public promenade lined with vintage lampposts and benches. Its wooden-plank pier, the city's longest, is ideal for fishing, eating a picnic lunch, or just gazing at boats. Another good spot is South Beach Harbor, just south of Pier 40, where you can check out the yachts and the views from south of the Bay Bridge. Whether you see it in spurts or all at once (Muni streetcars cover the whole distance), the Embarcadero offers an extravaganza of waterfront delights.

HEY, KIDS! At exactly 5:17 AM on April 18, 1906, the clock on the tower of the Ferry Building stopped dead—and didn't start up again for a year. Can you guess why? If you said "Because that's when the great San Francisco earthquake hit," take a bow.

KEEP IN MIND The new home of the San Francisco Giants, Pacific Bell Park (24 Willie Mays Plaza, between 2nd and 3rd Sts.) is at the foot of the Embarcadero. Modeled after the classic baseball-only stadiums of the past, Pac Bell, as it's called, is built right on the bay. Though individual tickets are scarce, the Giants hold out a few hundred seats for each game. To order, call 800/734-4268 or go online at www.sfgiants.com. You can also take a park tour ($10 ages 12 and up, $5 children 11 and under), offered daily 10–2 unless there's a game.

EXPLORATORIUM

Most kids' eyes light up as soon as they enter the Exploratorium. Set in the Marina District, it's one of the world's top science museums, drawing 600,000 visitors per year. More than 650 hands-on exhibits invite curious kids and parents to test and investigate mysteries of science and human perception—how we see, hear, smell, and feel the world around us. Light, color, sound, music, motion, language, electricity, and weather are among the subject areas.

What's that cloud ring rising into the air? A 5-year-old boy made it in the Weather area. How did that 7-year-old girl leave her shadow on the wall? Your kids can capture their own shadows in the Shadow Box. Look at that 10-year-old. He's as tall as the ceiling, but only in the Distorted Room. How did that family make the Enchanted Tree light up? Just by clapping their hands. Kids can try finger painting via computer, touch a miniature tornado, and blow giant soap bubbles, too. "Explainers"—often high-school students on their days off—offer help and demonstrations ("Cow-eye dissection starting over here!").

HEY, KIDS!
Some people say that entering the Tactile Dome is like being swallowed by a whale. The path inside is totally dark. It shows you how important your sense of touch really is and that this is one museum where it's "okay (even necessary) to touch."

EATS FOR KIDS The **Exploratorium Café** (tel. 415/921–8603) features such lunch items as organic salads and tuna or smoked turkey sandwiches for lunch. At noisy and colorful **Café Marimba** (2317 Chestnut St., tel. 415/776–1506), the Oaxacan-style Mexican food, served at lunch and dinner, includes family–size platters of grilled chicken or pork ribs, seafood tacos, and kid-pleasing quesadillas. **Bechelli's Restaurant** (2346 Chestnut St., tel. 415/346–1801) serves up breakfast and lunch daily at a horse-shoe–shape counter. Fare includes omelets, salads, burgers, and old-fashioned soda-fountain milkshakes.

3601 Lyon St., near Baker St. and Marina Blvd. (parking at Lyon and Bay Sts.)

415/397-5673, 415/561-0362 Tactile Dome; www.exploratorium.edu

 $9 adults, $7 college students, $5 youths 6–17, $2.50 children 3–5; 1st W of mth free

 Memorial Day–Labor Day, Th–T 10–6, W 10–9:30; early Sept–late May, T and Th–Su 10–5, W 10–9:30

2 and up

One of the newest areas, Playlab, is designed especially for infants and toddlers. Here they can play with blocks and develop motor skills on a climbing structure. The Exploratorium also features two or three intriguing temporary exhibits each year, exploring topics as varied as memory and flea circuses.

A separate area, the Tactile Dome, requires reservations (one to six weeks in advance), an additional fee, and a sense of adventure. In this pitch-black maze set inside a geodesic dome, the challenge—and the fun—is to crawl, slide, and climb through it relying entirely on your sense of touch. Kids should be at least 8 and not afraid of the dark; it's also not recommended for pregnant women or anyone who's claustrophobic. It takes about 15 minutes to work your way through once, but many inquisitive young explorers go through two or three times. By then your child will be ready to come back into the light and experience all five senses at this extraordinary museum.

KEEP IN MIND The Exploratorium is housed within the Palace of Fine Arts, a neoclassical domed and pillared beauty built for the 1915 Panama-Pacific International Exposition. It was intended to be temporary, but the city later decided it was too stunning to tear down, and it's the only structure still surviving from the exposition. The palace rises alongside a lovely tree-shaded lagoon occupied by mallards and swans, with benches and sloping grassy hillsides providing space for resting and sunning before or after visiting the museum.

FARALLON ISLAND NATURE CRUISE

44

On a clear day, from points along the western edges of San Francisco, you can usually see the Farallon Islands jutting up from the Pacific, 27 miles off the Golden Gate. Even most longtime San Franciscans, however, have never seen the Farallones close up—or have a clue as to the extraordinary display of wildlife that's out there. The seven islands, comprising the Farallon National Wildlife Refuge, are home to 23 species of marine mammals, including thousands of harbor seals, California sea lions, Steller's sea lions, and Northern elephant seals. And up to 300,000 breeding seabirds visit the islands annually, making this the largest Pacific seabird rookery south of Alaska.

Only small groups of researchers are allowed on the refuge at a time. The public isn't allowed to set foot in this fragile environment, sometimes called "the most exclusive neighborhood in San Francisco" (the islands are within city and county limits). But you can get excellent views of the islands' rocky slopes from the deck of an Oceanic Society Expeditions boat.

KEEP IN MIND This is a trip you definitely need to prepare for ahead of time. Make sure everyone in your family dresses warmly and waterproofed, since trips depart rain or shine. Be certain of your children's seaworthiness before embarking, as there's no turning back. Kids should have sailed on the ocean at least once before going. Take seasickness precautions, and bring binoculars, sunglasses, and sunscreen, even if the weather is foggy at departure. (You're less likely to encounter foggy weather in fall than in summer.)

Oceanic Society Expeditions,
Ft. Mason Center, Bldg. E

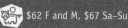 $62 F and M, $67 Sa–Su

 Departures June–Nov, F–Su 8:30 AM

 415/474–3385, 800/326–7491;
www.oceanic-society.org

10 and up

The eight-hour Farallon Island Nature Cruise (reservations required), aboard a 63-foot Coast Guard–certified vessel, departs from San Francisco's Ft. Mason (*see* #30). The trip is for adults and children 10 and over only, since the seas can get rough and the winds very cold. Expert naturalists point out wildlife and answer questions. As you set out past the Golden Gate, you and your children may spot such birds as gulls, murres, pelicans, oystercatchers, albatrosses, and tufted puffins. Chances are a number of Dall porpoises will escort the boat, darting around, past, and under the bow in a sort of exhilarating joyride. Whales are a common sight: humpbacks with flukes shooting high in the air as they dive, and even blue whales, the largest mammals ever on earth. Pacific white-sided or Risso's dolphins sometimes surface, too. The granite islands themselves are alive with birds, their shrieking and squawking surrounding you in natural stereo, while a parcel of barking sea lions typically provides the basso profundo. It's one "concert" your kids aren't likely to forget.

HEY, KIDS! Keep a sharp eye out for whales spouting (the spouts look like puffs of smoke), which often means they're about to surface. If you spot one, let the naturalist on board know about it, so he or she can alert the other passengers.

EATS FOR KIDS You'll need to bring snacks, lunch, and drinks for the boat trip since there's no galley on board. For dinner, **Greens** (Ft. Mason Center, Bldg. A, tel. 415/771–6222) is an excellent vegetarian restaurant, good for older kids. It has terrific bay views, but you'll need reservations. **Mels Drive-In** (2165 Lombard St., tel. 415/921–2867) serves up burgers, curly fries, milk shakes, and cherry Cokes with '50s decor and jukeboxes. Kids' meals come in toy Corvettes. **Café Marimba** (*see* #45) serves creative Mexican cuisine.

FISHERMAN'S WHARF

Fisherman's Wharf is no longer the thriving fishing center it was a century ago. Modern-day catches have been ravaged by overfishing and pollution. Today, the historic waterfront district, a now loosely defined area that runs for eight or nine blocks from Aquatic Park to Pier 39 (*see* #18), relies mainly on tourism for revenues. Crowds can be overwhelming (come in the morning if possible), and the last remnants of the real working wharf can be hard to find amid the hodgepodge of attractions—some maritime related, some not, and many overpriced. These include schlocky souvenir stands, novelty museums, and often-mediocre seafood restaurants. For all these reasons, many locals avoid it. Still, the bay sparkles, boats are near at hand, you can get here by cable car, and it's a colorful, noisy, active place that kids tend to like.

GETTING THERE

Though there are public parking lots near the Wharf, you'll pay dearly for most of them. It's cheaper (and more fun) to take public transportation. You can ride the Powell–Hyde or Powell–Taylor cable cars, or take the F Line's historic Muni trolleys up the Embarcadero.

To glimpse real fishermen at work, head for Richard Henry Dana Street (better known as "Fish Alley"), but remember that fishermen work early. Some other authentic sights at the Wharf are provided on a bevy of historic ships berthed there. The Hyde Street Pier

KEEP IN MIND Though many of the Wharf's commercial attractions are tourist traps, that doesn't mean kids don't enjoy them. One of the better ones is a branch of Ripley's Believe It or Not! Museum (175 Jefferson St., tel. 415/771–6188), which chronicles the bizarre and unusual with oddities such as a shrunken human torso, an 8-foot-long cable car built from matchsticks, and a portrait of Rudolph Valentino made from dryer lint. Another is the newly expanded Wax Museum at Fisherman's Wharf (145 Jefferson St., tel. 800/439–4305), which includes the slightly gruesome Chamber of Horrors.

Bounded by Aquatic Park, North Point,
Powell St., and Pier 39

Free; some
attractions charge

Daily 24 hours; attractions shorter hrs

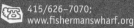
415/626–7070;
www.fishermanswharf.org

5 and up

(*see* #38) includes a fascinating collection of boats, and you can tour two World War II vessels berthed at Pier 45 (*see* #34).

Free entertainment is often here, too, in the form of street performers—jugglers, musicians, magicians—one of the best bargains around even if you drop some coins in their hats. You can usually find them on sidewalks or at the area's four main shopping centers: the Cannery, Ghirardelli Square, Pier 39, and the Anchorage. The Cannery began as the world's largest peach-canning plant in 1907; Ghirardelli Square was once a chocolate factory. Today, both open-air complexes have specialty shops, restaurants, and galleries, and the Cannery has a minibranch of the Basic Brown Bear Factory (*see* #63). Like everywhere else at the Wharf, you'll have plenty of company here from other families, who come from around the world to soak up the atmosphere—and try to avoid bumping into each other.

EATS FOR KIDS It's hard to resist the stands with bubbling **crab pots** on Jefferson Street for a crab or shrimp cocktail, even if many are skimpy for the price. Two good fish restaurants are **A. Sabella's** (2766 Taylor St., tel. 415/771–6775), which serves seafood and pasta with an extensive children's menu, and **Alioto's** (8 Fisherman's Wharf, tel. 415/673–0183), with old-time atmosphere and seafood that really does match the views. For details about the **Ghirardelli Chocolate Manufactory and Soda Fountain,** see #38.

FT. FUNSTON

42

Where's the fort at Ft. Funston? You won't find a walled fortress or cannons here. The military did, however, once stake a claim to this area of windswept sands just south of Ocean Beach (see #20), along the western reaches of San Francisco.

Since the early 1900s, and through two world wars, the Army used the high cliffs at Ft. Funston as a strategic lookout and a base for heavy weaponry protecting San Francisco Bay from attack. During World War II, Ft. Funston's Battery Davis sported guns weighing almost 150 tons each. During the Cold War, the current parking lot was the site of a Nike missile battery. But since the Army pulled out some years ago, all that remains of its legacy are gun emplacements gathering rust in the foggy mists.

Today, Ft. Funston is part of the Golden Gate National Recreation Area, and where guns once pointed out to the Pacific, rangers and volunteers now run a nursery for native plants and lead environmental education programs for schoolkids. What's more, the last of the

EATS FOR KIDS There are picnic tables but no food concessions here, and though there are no eating places in the immediate vicinity of Ft. Funston, you can find some a few minutes' drive away. Among the closest are the **Boathouse** (see #36) and those across from the San Francisco Zoo on Sloat Boulevard. Tiny **Leon's Bar-B-Q** (2800 Sloat Blvd., tel. 415/681–3071) dishes up ribs, jambalaya, and sweet-potato pie in casual surroundings. For details on **John's Ocean Beach Cafe,** see #10.

Skyline Blvd. off Great Hwy.
or John Muir Dr.

Free

Daily 6 AM–10 PM, visitor
center center Sa–Su 12–4

415/556–8371, 415/333–0100
weather hot line for hang gliders

5 and up

undeveloped dunes that once blanketed much of the coast are still preserved here. You and your children can hike to the beach below or watch from a viewing deck as hang gliders take off from the cliffs and soar through the skies. The Sunset Trail, a 1-mile paved loop that links up to the Coastal Trail going north along Ocean Beach, traverses the cliffs and provides sea views. As its name suggests, this is one of the best places in San Francisco to watch the sun go down—at least when it's not clouded with coastal fog. Stay on marked trails: Some of the roads you may see here actually go nowhere. They were built to confuse the enemy in wartime, but thankfully, no enemies ever invaded. And Ft. Funston remains enough off the beaten track that crowds never invade here, either. It makes for a nice spot to wander among dunes and enjoy nature without leaving the city.

KEEP IN MIND
Though rare, crashes have occurred at the hang-gliding observation deck, so it's a good idea to keep an eye out—and up. Some other safety suggestions: In general, keep your kids away from cliff edges, dress warmly, and beware of riptides at the beach.

HEY, KIDS! Much of the vegetation—ice plant, acacia, eucalyptus, and Monterey cypress trees—that you see along the trail was planted here by the Army to provide camouflage, or disguise, for the gun batteries at Ft. Funston as well as to control soil erosion. Rangers are now trying to get rid of some of it to make room for native plants, like sticky monkey flower and beach sagewort. Wondering what those funny-sounding plants look like? Check out the greenhouse near the visitor center to see.

FT. POINT NATIONAL HISTORIC SITE

Dramatically situated beneath the southern stretches of the Golden Gate Bridge on San Francisco Bay, Ft. Point is the only brick fort you can visit in the western United States. Built during the Civil War to help protect San Francisco from sea attack—it was modeled after Ft. Sumter in South Carolina and completed in 1861—the massive fort could hold as many as 500 soldiers and 126 cannons. During World War II, soldiers stood watch here as part of the coastal defense of California. Today it's part of Presidio National Park (*see #16*) and a good place to immerse kids in some local military history while soaking up breathtaking vistas of the bay below and the bridge overhead.

The best views are from the roof of the fort, where your kids can pretend they're searching for enemy ships. More likely, they'll spot windsurfers braving the waves here or freighters passing through the Golden Gate. Just to the east, where the surf crashes into the rocks below the walkway, is the spot where Jimmy Stewart pulled Kim Novak out of the water in the Hitchcock film *Vertigo* (a good video to watch with older kids before visiting).

KEEP IN MIND The Presidio's "new" Crissy Field lies just to the east of Ft. Point along the bay. After two years of restoring native plants and dunes, the National Park Service reopened this shoreline park in 2001, with beach access and trails for walkers, cyclists, runners, and skaters.

HEY, KIDS! When the rangers ask for volunteers to help load the cannons, you might want to join in. If you do, you'll receive a special cannoneer certificate. You don't need to worry about getting hit by a cannonball—or even loud noises—since the cannons aren't actually fired, and no live ammo is used. Volunteers each do one job, such as cleaning the cannon, loading the charge, relaying the ammo, and firing—well, actually only pretending to fire. All ages are welcome to help out.

Marine Dr. off Long Ave.
and Lincoln Blvd., the Presidio

 Free

W–Su 10–5

415/556–1693; www.nps.gov/fopo

6 and up

Even though Ft. Point was well equipped with cannons, none have ever been fired in anger here. But national park rangers conduct cannon-loading demonstrations on an 1862-era field artillery piece every day, and it's a complex, fascinating process. (Call the fort for the daily schedule.) Sometimes, on busy weekends and holidays, docents dressed in Civil War–era costumes give tours, adding to the historical flavor. Your family can also visit the rooms that lie off the restored central courtyard to see museum-style exhibits of American military memorabilia and watch a film containing old newsreel footage of the building of the Golden Gate Bridge. In addition, rangers lead weekend walking tours of Ft. Point and other former military installations in the Presidio—best for kids 10 and up. The outing is both informative and entertaining, the site strategic and stunning.

EATS FOR KIDS Crissy Field and other areas of the Presidio make nice picnic spots. The Presidio's branch of **Burger King** (211 Lincoln Blvd., tel. 415/673–1856) is like any other Burger King except that it has one of the best views of the Golden Gate Bridge of any restaurant in the city. It's also the closest eating place to Ft. Point. For restaurants in the nearby Richmond District (follow Lincoln Boulevard west to 25th Avenue), see #56; for Marina District eateries, just east of the Presidio, see #45.

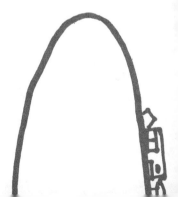

GOLDEN GATE BRIDGE

It's the symbol of San Francisco and probably the most celebrated and photographed bridge in the world. Completed in 1937 after four years of construction, the Golden Gate Bridge is still one of the world's longest suspension bridges, stretching across the straits (aka the Golden Gate) from San Francisco north to Marin County. Its two towers rise 750 feet into the air, and it uses enough cable wire to wrap around the equator three times. More than 40 million vehicles cross it each year. You can drive across the bridge, too, of course, but the best way to see it—and the views from it—is to walk across.

Pedestrians can ride the No. 28 or 29 Muni bus to the bridge and get off at the toll plaza. If you drive, park your car either at the lot on the San Francisco side or at Vista Point, on the Marin side, and set out on foot along the walkway that runs along the eastern (bay side) of the bridge. Bring plenty of quarters for the parking meters and make sure everyone dresses warmly, even on sunny days, because the winds can whip fiercely across the bridge and you never know when the damp fog will come swirling in. Though the bridge is 1.7

KEEP IN MIND If your kids are old enough and good cyclists, you can ride bikes across the bridge. Bikers are limited to the west (ocean) side of the bridge on weekends and weekday evenings. Experienced cyclists might consider continuing to Sausalito, in Marin County, for more bay-side views or to explore the town. Just follow the bike lane at the end of the Vista Point parking lot to Alexander Avenue, but realize that once off the bridge, you'll be sharing the road with cars.

Hwy. 1 and U.S. 101 north (from Marina, take Doyle Dr. from Marina Blvd.)

 Pedestrians, bikes, and northbound cars free; southbound cars $3

 Daily 24 hrs bikes and cars, 5 AM–9 PM pedestrians

415/921-5858;
www.goldengatebridge.org

4 and up

miles long (including approaches), you don't need to cover the full distance to get the full effect. It's a thrill just to get a few hundred feet out onto the bridge, which stands 220 feet above the water. You'll feel the rush of air as cars whiz by and feel the bridge sway in the wind. In fact, it can sway as much as 27½ feet east to west.

Linger as long as you want—and as your kids will allow—to see the views of the city skyline, Alcatraz, Angel Island, Ft. Point, the Marin Headlands, and a passing parade of sailboats, freighters, and windsurfers. Times when fog is swirling about are especially magical, but whenever you go, it's an unforgettable experience.

EATS FOR KIDS
The closest San Francisco restaurants are in the Richmond and Marina districts. **Giorgio's Pizzeria** (151 Clement St., tel. 415/668-1266), in the Richmond, is a longtime contender for the city's best pizza. For other options, see #45.

HEY, KIDS! When you're walking on the bridge, look up toward the cables to try to spot painters on the walkways. The bridge takes four years to paint—a process that never ends. As soon as they finish, they start all over again, using up 5,000 gallons of paint every year. Some kids—and adults, too—are surprised that the bridge isn't painted gold to match its name. Its reddish-orange color, called "International Orange," was chosen because it's easiest to see in the fog, helping planes and birds avoid collisions.

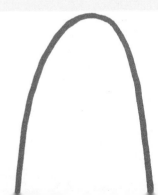

GOLDEN GATE PARK

You could probably spend every weekend for a year in 3-mile-long, ½-mile-wide Golden Gate Park and still miss at least one corner of it. Though fraying a bit around the edges—cutbacks in public funds mean fewer gardeners and maintenance people and more homeless "campers"—this remains one of America's most beautiful urban parks, filled with lakes, flowers, and meadows.

Most attractions are clustered in the eastern half of the park, including the outstanding California Academy of Sciences (*see* #57). In front of the museum is the Music Concourse, where the park band plays free concerts on Sunday afternoons. Just down the road is the Japanese Tea Garden, with arched bridges, koi fish ponds, and a towering red pagoda. Across from the Tea Garden, Strybing Arboretum & Botanical Gardens displays flowers, redwoods, cacti, and other flora from around the world; don't miss the duck pond near the entrance.

Just up Martin Luther King Jr. Drive is pretty Stow Lake, where you can picnic and rent

HEY, KIDS!

Chances are you've had fortune cookies at a Chinese restaurant, but did you know they weren't invented in China or Japan? In fact, a lot of people think the first ones were served right here in Golden Gate Park—at the Japanese Tea Garden—around 1920.

KEEP IN MIND If you like to bike or go rollerblading with your kids, the best time to visit Golden Gate Park is on Sundays, when Kennedy Drive is closed to cars between Stanyan Street and 19th Avenue and cyclists and rollerbladers take over. At 6th Avenue and Fulton Street, a flat paved area draws flashy skaters who jump and do dance steps to lively music. In all, the park has more than 7 miles of paved roads and trails to follow. A number of places nearby rent bikes and skates.

Bounded by Fulton and Stanyan Sts., Lincoln Way, and Great Hwy.

 Free; some attractions charge

415/831–2700, 415/752–4227 Japanese Tea Garden

Daily 6 AM–10 PM

All ages

rowboats, paddleboats, or electric boats. With older kids, cross footbridges to hilly Strawberry Island, in the middle of the lake, and hike to the top to peer over the crest of Huntington Falls, which plunges 125 feet—the West's highest artificial waterfall. Nearby, the Rhododendron Dell blazes with color in spring. In the park's southeast corner, younger kids flock to the Children's Playground (off Kezar or Bowling Green Drs.), which contains swings, slides, and climbing structures; the adjacent 1912 Herschel-Spillman Carousel spins with 62 hand-carved animals. The park's western half is more woodsy and pastoral. Toward the ocean (along Kennedy Drive), you can visit a herd of bison at the Bison Paddock and hike, bike, or stroll along quiet tree-lined trails.

The park also contains horse trails and stables, a par-3 golf course, tennis courts, horseshoe pits, lawn-bowling greens, handball courts, ball fields, fly-casting pools, dog runs, a polo field, and an archery field. Come to think of it, you could spend every weekend in the park and still miss *several* corners of it.

EATS FOR KIDS Picnic spots abound in the park. Some of the best include Stow Lake, the Strybing Arboretum, and the various meadows along John F. Kennedy Drive west of 19th Avenue. Staff in traditional costume serve tea and cookies at the **Teahouse** (Japanese Tea Garden, Tea Garden Dr., tel. 415/752–1171). For more restaurants on the fringes of the park, such as the **Canvas, Park Chow, Louis',** and the **Beach Chalet,** see #57, #49, and #20.

HYDE STREET PIER

This pier, part of the San Francisco Maritime National Historic Park, is the site of the world's largest fleet of historic ships (by tonnage) and the country's only floating national park. This is a great spot to introduce kids to what shipboard life was like in the days before *The Love Boat* or even the *Titanic*.

The *Balclutha*, an 1886 steel-hulled, square-rigged sailing ship, is the flagship vessel. The 300-foot-long windjammer was launched in Scotland and navigated Cape Horn 17 times before ending its days transporting Alaskan salmon from the Bering Sea to San Francisco (when it was known as the *Star of Alaska*). Kids usually enjoy clambering down its narrow ladders and around its claustrophobic decks for looks at its restored cabins. Several other ships are also on display. The *C.A. Thayer* is a three-masted schooner built in 1895 to move the lumber that helped build many early California cities. San Francisco Bay's oldest ferry, the paddle wheeler *Eureka*, dates from 1890 and was once the world's largest auto and passenger ferry. The 1891 scow schooner *Alma* has a flat bottom that enabled her to navigate

HEY, KIDS! Imagine the scene before the Golden Gate and Bay bridges made it possible for people to drive across San Francisco Bay. In the early 20th century, thousands of passengers boarded the *Eureka* every day to ride to Marin County, Oakland, or Berkeley. The *Eureka* also served as "the tracks across the bay," as it carried passengers on the final leg of their train journeys across the United States. The trains stopped at Oakland, and the ferry then took them to San Francisco. That was long before BART engineers figured out how to run trains *under* the water.

Foot of Hyde St.; museum, foot of Polk St.

 Pier $5 adults, $2 children 12–17; museum free

 Pier daily 9:30–5, museum daily 10–5

415/556–3002, 415/556–0859 tickets; www.nps.gov/safr

 4 and up; museum 6 and up

the shallow waters on the periphery of the bay, where she hauled hay. And the *Hercules* is a steam-powered ocean tug that is boardable at high tide only. Special family events—sail-raisings, sea chantey songfests, evening concerts—are held here periodically.

If you have some extra time and school-age kids along, consider stopping into the National Maritime Museum, housed in a 1930s Art Deco building and part of the national historic park. Highlights include a collection of intricately crafted ship models along with rows of carved figureheads that once adorned the bows of Gold Rush–era clippers. Photos, maps, diaries, and ships' logs help chronicle West Coast maritime history. There's a real bonus to visiting this area: The Powell-Hyde cable car terminus is right above Hyde Street Pier. What better way to get kids in the mood for exploring 19th-century ships than riding 19th-century cable cars to get there?

KEEP IN MIND Aquatic Park (tel. 415/556–1238), just below the National Maritime Museum, is a good place to relax after touring the ships or museum. Kids can wade in the gentle (though cold) water at a sandy beach. The Municipal Pier, a favored fishing spot, is nearby.

EATS FOR KIDS You can spread out a blanket and picnic at Aquatic Park, where you can also find snack bars. Just above the park, at the popular Ghirardelli Square shopping complex (North Point St.), the **Ghirardelli Chocolate Manufactory and Soda Fountain** (tel. 415/474–3938) draws hordes of families who come to gorge on huge sundaes, floats, and other chocolate concoctions. (Lines can be brutally long at peak tourist hours.) You can still watch chocolate being made in original vats and ovens in the old-fashioned ice-cream parlor. For area fish restaurants, see #43.

JAPANTOWN

Japantown is the focal point for San Francisco's residents of Japanese descent, who first settled this area after the 1906 earthquake. As the Japanese built churches, shrines, shops, and restaurants, the neighborhood began to take on the look of a miniature Ginza and became known as Nihonmachi or Japantown. Its commercial heart is the Japan Center (Post and Buchanan Sts.)—a three-square-block complex of shops, restaurants, teahouses, hotels, pastry shops, movie theaters, Japanese baths, and more, all connected by walkways. With the exception of a five-tiered, 100-foot-high pagoda crowning its Peace Plaza, a few fountains, and other touches, the Japan Center's design lacks traditional Japanese grace. But it's a fun place for kids to wander around, perhaps eyeing the plastic food displays in restaurant windows, shopping for CDs, or leafing through Japanese books. They can also look for flying-fish kites, miniature notepads, and other colorful items from Japan in the shops.

A 135-foot covered bridge lined with shops and a restaurant crosses over Webster Street

KEEP IN MIND Street parking is difficult, but the Japan Center has two big indoor parking garages. Most stores, restaurants, and theaters will validate parking. Alternately, take Muni's No. 38 Geary bus, which runs between Union Square and the Richmond District and stops at Japantown.

HEY, KIDS! Though the Japantown area bustles with people today, during World War II it was mostly deserted. That's because the United States, which was at war with Japan then, moved many Japanese-Americans to prison-like internment camps elsewhere in the state, fearing that people of Japanese origin might side with Japan over this country. Many of these people had been born here and were American citizens, yet both their freedom and their property were taken away during the war. The United States was also at war with Germany but did not treat German-Americans that way. Do you think the country did the right thing?

Bounded by Geary Blvd. and
Fillmore, Laguna, and Bush Sts.

 Free

Most shops daily 10–6,
Japan Center daily 10–10

415/922–6776 Japan Center,
415/563–2313 Cherry Blossom Festival;
japantown.citysearch.com

 6 and up

between two of the commercial buildings. It's a wonderful spot to browse, as is the Buchanan Mall, which runs for a block along Buchanan Street between Sutter and Post streets. More attractive than the Japan Center, it's a pedestrian-only mall with cobbled streets, flowering plum and cherry trees, and several restaurants.

The highlight of the year in Japantown is the Nihonmachi Cherry Blossom Festival, held during two weekends each April. Traditional Japanese dancing, often by kids in colorful kimonos, along with fast-paced martial arts demonstrations are presented on an outdoor stage at the Japan Center. There's also a food bazaar and a special Children's Village with arts, crafts, and games. A dazzling, 2½-hour parade—running 15 blocks from City Hall to the Japan Center—caps the second weekend. It stars dancers, floats, samurai warriors, *taiko* drummers, shrine bearers, and the festival queen—that's right, not an empress, but nonetheless all very Japanese.

EATS FOR KIDS Though other types of food *are* available, the idea of going to Japantown and not eating Japanese food seems positively un-American. **Mifune** (Kintetsu Bldg., 1737 Post St., Japan Center, tel. 415/922–0337) has tasty, inexpensive noodle dishes, including children's plates. At **Isobune Sushi** (Kintetsu Bldg., 1737 Post St., Japan Center, tel. 415/563–1030), you can pluck the sushi of your choice from little boats as they float around the counter, but every piece that's plucked must be paid for, so make sure your kids choose only what they can eat.

LAKE MERCED

Until sand dunes severed its narrow link to the Pacific about a century ago, this pretty lake in the far southwestern corner of San Francisco was an ocean-side lagoon. Freshwater has replaced saltwater, and Lake Merced now serves as an emergency city reservoir. But it's long been known as a recreational mecca, traditionally providing some of the best and most accessible fishing, boating, picnicking, bicycling, and running in the city. One of San Francisco's top public golf courses, tree-shaded Harding Park, also lies along its shores.

Lake Merced has 7 miles of shoreline, bordered much of the way by tule rushes and frequented by migratory birds. A moderately level path that's a favorite of cyclists, skaters, runners, and walkers loops around the lake. The path is partly shaded by eucalyptus, cypress, and pine trees; wildflowers, ferns, and berry bushes also line the route.

A narrow isthmus cuts the lake almost in two, with the larger southern portion more popular

HEY, KIDS! Back in 1859, Lake Merced—or at least the lake's shoreline—was the scene of one of the city's most famous duels. (These were usually prearranged gun battles, popular in the 19th century, to resolve some "point of honor.") In this case, the two combatants were none other than the Chief Justice of the California Supreme Court, David Terry, and a United States Senator, David Broderick. No one knows for sure if their fight was over politics or personal matters, but we do know that the judge shot the senator, who died three days later. It makes today's political squabbles look pretty tame.

Sloat, Skyline, Lake Merced, and Sunset Blvds.

 Free

 Daily 24 hrs; boat rental and bait shop, daily sunrise–sunset

415/831–2700 park, 415/681–3310 boat rental, 415/664–4690 golf

 6 and up

for boating. You can rent rowboats, paddleboats, canoes, kayaks, and boats with electric motors or take sailing lessons from the Lake Merced Boating and Fishing Company. (Rowboats, the cheapest, are $12 per hour, $25 for a full day.) The Lake Merced Boating and Fishing Company also rents rods and reels ($8 per day) and other fishing equipment. The waters here are stocked with trout. In fact, the lake has long been one of the top spots for year-round fishing in the Bay Area, known for introducing countless young people to the sport. In recent years, however, water levels in the lake have been dropping, and the trout-fishing prospects have dropped with it. Some activist groups suspect neighboring golf courses may be siphoning water and fear the beloved lake may become more like a shallow swamp. Stay tuned. It promises to become a hot environmental controversy. So besides a peaceful urban respite, Lake Merced has now become a place to help educate kids about the need to preserve what we often take for granted.

KEEP IN MIND
If you do fish here, remember that kids 15 and under don't require a fishing license, but those 12 and over do need a daily fishing permit, which costs 95¢–$4. Licenses cost $9.70 per day or $27.05 for a year.

EATS FOR KIDS Picnic tables and barbecue grills are situated around the lake—many in a grassy area near the Boathouse. In addition, the boat-rental concession sells snacks. The **Boathouse** (1 Harding Park Rd., tel. 415/681–2727), on the road to the golf course and surrounded on two sides by lake, has a sports-bar atmosphere and can get rowdy on football Sundays. Nevertheless, it serves kid-friendly food like hot dogs and chicken nuggets. Other nearby restaurants are on Sloat Boulevard (see #42 and #10).

LAWRENCE HALL OF SCIENCE

Nestled up a winding road high in the Berkeley hills, this museum was built as a memorial to Ernest O. Lawrence, the University of California at Berkeley's first Nobel prize–winning laureate and an inventor of the atomic bomb. It's loaded with interactive exhibits geared mostly toward children, which can entertain them for hours. Big hands-on displays and flashy special exhibitions are typical here. The emphasis is on biology, chemistry, and astronomy.

Before you enter, you may want to linger in the outer courtyard to let your children clamber over the 60-foot-long model of DNA, while you enjoy panoramic views of San Francisco Bay. Or take a short walk up the nearby hillside to find the wind organ, a set of 36 long, slender pipes sticking out of the ground. You and your kids will hear music if you walk among them when the wind is blowing. You can also play with their tones by turning one of six moveable pipes.

GETTING THERE From I-80/580, take the University Avenue exit and go 2 miles to Oxford Street. Go left on Oxford and then right on Hearst Avenue. Take another right on Gayley Road, a left on Stadium Rimway, and another left on Centennial Drive. Follow that 1 mile uphill to the museum.

KEEP IN MIND On the first and third Saturday evenings of each month 8–11, you can stargaze with your family (even though the museum is closed). Astronomers bring their telescopes to give interested visitors a free peek at the moon, planets, star clusters, and galaxies. Call the hall and select the astronomy information option for tips on what constellations, eclipses, and such you and your kids can see in the sky on a particular night.

Centennial Dr. near Grizzly
Peak Blvd., Berkeley

 510/642–5132;
www.lhs.berkeley.edu

 $7 adults, $5 youths
5–18, $3 children 3–4;
planetarium $2

 Daily 10–5

3 and up

Inside, permanent exhibitions include Within the Human Brain (you can even watch a video of a human brain dissection) and Science View Vision, all about the eye and how we see. The Earthquakes exhibit contains a working seismograph and tips on surviving the Big One. YEA! (Young Explorers Area), for preschoolers, has puppets, blocks, books, and an insect zoo. Temporary exhibits tackle topics like the science of toys.

Some activities—such as the Biology Discovery Lab, where kids can pet a snake or hold a tarantula, along with computer labs, Holt Planetarium shows, films, lectures, and laboratory demonstrations—are available only in summer or on weekends and holidays. (Most planetarium shows are for kids 8 and older, but there are special shows for ages 4 and up.) In addition, the museum hosts periodic Family Days—which include outdoor concerts, picnics, and art and science activities—as well as family workshops and classes. So no matter how many times you visit, chances are good there'll always be something new here to do and see.

EATS FOR KIDS The museum's **Small Planet Café** (tel. 510/644–1880) serves hot dogs, soups, sandwiches, and salads. You can also picnic at nearby Tilden Park (see #5), or drive back down out of the hills to eat at **Fat Apple's** (1346 Martin Luther King Jr., Blvd., tel. 510/526–2260), where the burgers always draw big crowds. For kids with more adventurous tastes, try **Cha Am** (1543 Shattuck Ave., tel. 510/848–9664), where pad thai and other tasty Thai dishes are served at bargain prices.

LIBERTY SHIP *JEREMIAH O'BRIEN*

During World War II, some two-thirds of America's fleet of more than 2,700 Liberty Ships were built in the Bay Area. (The Liberty Ships were part of a merchant fleet designed to carry troops and wartime supplies including tanks and planes across the oceans and took part in landings ranging from Normandy to Guadalcanal.) Ironically, the U.S.S. *Jeremiah O'Brien* was built in Oregon. But more than a half century later, the *Jeremiah O'Brien*—the only Liberty Ship to remain afloat and in its original condition—is now integrally associated with San Francisco, berthed at Pier 45 at Fisherman's Wharf.

The city, and the entire area, embraced the gray-hulled ship and its history when, in 1994, it was restored and sailed by volunteers across the Atlantic to mark the 50th anniversary of D-Day, for which it had ferried troops. In fact, it was the only U.S. vessel to both take part in the Normandy invasion and return for the anniversary. Most of the Liberty Ships were sold off after World War II or scrapped after Vietnam; about 200 were sunk during World War II.

KEEP IN MIND Another authentic World War II vessel is anchored at Pier 45, this one a restored submarine. Launched in 1943, the U.S.S. *Pampanito* (tel. 415/775–1943) saw action in the Pacific, sank six enemy warships, and rescued 73 allied POWs. Self-guided audio tours lead through the cramped crews' and officers' quarters, the engine rooms, and the torpedo room. Admission is $7 for ages 13 and up, $4 for children 6–12. It's open daily 9–6, and Memorial Day–Labor Day, until 8.

Pier 45 (foot of Taylor St.)

$6 ages 14 and up, $3 children 6–13

Daily 9–5

415/441–3101

6 and up

Today, the entire ship maintains its 1940s appearance. You and your children can walk the decks, where antiaircraft guns (no longer loaded, of course) remain on vigil, and then go below to explore the mazelike corridors, the sailors' quarters, the radio operator's room, and the bridge.

For a really claustrophobic experience, descend to the vessel's lower level and into the depths of the boiler room, where the enormous engines (which appeared in the movie *Titanic*) are still in working order. The engines are tuned up on periodic "steaming weekends," when they're operated dockside. These are essential because the ship makes twice-yearly bay cruises, around Memorial Day and during Fleet Week in October. You and your family can come aboard for $100 a person (same price for adults and kids; call for reservations). But if that's too extravagant, don't worry: You can still have fun here any day of the year.

EATS FOR KIDS
For burgers, fries, and shakes, try **Johnny Rockets** (81 Jefferson St., tel. 415/693–9120). The **Rainforest Café** (145 Jefferson St., tel. 415/440–5610) has an entertaining tropical theme and decent, if overpriced, food. For other local eateries, see #43, #38, and #18.

HEY, KIDS! Guess how long it took to build the *Jeremiah O'Brien*. Remember that it's huge: 441 feet long and weighing 7,176 tons. If you guessed "just under two months," give yourself an award. Many Liberty Ships were built even faster—in just a month or so—and one was built in only four days! (It helped that they all used the same design.) The ships were needed quickly to carry cargo during World War II, and building them fast was considered more important than building them to last. Maybe that's why the *Jeremiah O'Brien* is the only Liberty Ship still afloat.

LINDSAY WILDLIFE MUSEUM

The centerpiece of this East Bay museum, founded in 1955, is the nation's oldest and one of its largest wildlife rehabilitation centers. The Lindsay treats more than 6,000 injured or orphaned animals each year, representing 200 different species mostly native to California—among them bald eagles, hawks, owls, bobcats, coyotes, foxes, snakes, and rabbits. A bald eagle, for instance, may have become entangled in a power line. A hawk may have crashed into a home's window. An owl may have flown into the path of a car. Wildlife officers bring them in, as do hikers and homeowners. Nearly half are eventually returned to the wild. Those creatures too sick, injured, or tame to survive on their own may be put on display at the museum—a sparkling facility that was expanded and remodeled in 1994.

Don't think of the Lindsay as a zoo, though. Its goal is not to show off the animals but to teach the public about California wildlife, the impact of human activity on it, and how the needs of people can be balanced with those of wild animals. Daily presentations

EATS FOR KIDS Larkey Park has picnic tables, and downtown Walnut Creek's North Main Street, about a mile from the museum, has many family-friendly eateries, including **Lyon's** (1750 N. Main St., tel. 925/935–4666), a coffee shop, and **Fuddruckers** (1940 N. Main St., tel. 925/943–1450), where burgers are king.

HEY, KIDS! Of the animals brought into the wildlife hospital here, almost a third have been injured by cats. Most of them are birds, such as robins, jays, and hummingbirds. Small mammals such as squirrels and opossums and reptiles such as lizards and turtles are other common patients. If you find an injured bird or other animal, don't try to feed or handle it. Keep it in a cardboard box with a lid, in a quiet, dark place, until you and your parents can bring it to the hospital.

Larkey Park, 1931 1st Ave.,
Walnut Creek

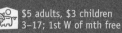
$5 adults, $3 children
3–17; 1st W of mth free

Mid-June–Aug, T–Su 10–5; Sept–mid-
June, T–F 12–5, Sa–Su 10–5

925/935–1978;
www.wildlife-museum.org

2 and up

allow closer looks at certain animals, and you can watch as some are fed. But there's nothing flashy or cute here: The animals don't do tricks, you can't pet the wild creatures, and staff members don't pretend that the animals want to be here.

A number of exhibits are geared toward young children. In the Discovery Room, your youngsters can explore a scale model of a backyard that may be similar to your own and hunt for animals—an opossum, a squirrel, a screech owl, a bat, a raccoon—that make themselves at home here. The difference is that these animals aren't alive; they've visited the taxidermist. The Lindsay also offers a wide variety of classes for all ages at the museum and beyond, some using live animals. But however you use the Lindsay, chances are your kids will come away with a greater understanding that wildlife protection begins at home.

KEEP IN MIND If you live locally and pay for a museum membership ($50), your kids can use the Lindsay's Pet Library Program. This lets them check out a live domestic (not wild) rabbit, guinea pig, hamster, or rat for one week. These animals were once pets, but their former families couldn't keep them. It's a good way to find out if your kids are ready to have a pet full-time themselves or to just enjoy caring for one temporarily. Kids must be at least 6, and 10 for a rabbit.

LOMBARD STREET

Officially, it's the 1000 block of Lombard Street, but everybody knows it as "the Crookedest Street in the World." (The end of Vermont Street on Potrero Hill may actually be *more* crooked, but it's way off the beaten path.) Lombard's eight hairpin curves, which zigzag down the east face of Russian Hill, are some of the most heavily driven, and photographed, stretches of roadway in existence.

To best appreciate Lombard Street, you'll need a car. At the intersection of Hyde and Lombard—where you may well encounter a mini-traffic jam—begin your snake-like drive down the red-cobblestone-lined street. It's impossible, really, to take it anything but slow or (for the driver) to do anything but steer back and forth. Kids usually love the ride. Have them count the curves as you go down, and to make it a real surprise, don't tell them where they're going before starting down. Chances are your car will show up in countless other people's photographs as you'll probably see scads of picture-snapping tourists both at the beginning and the end of the block.

HEY, KIDS! If you want to ride down another of San Francisco's steepest streets, ask your parents to take you to Filbert Street between Hyde and Leavenworth—just two blocks from the Crookedest Street. This one has a 31.5% grade but no switchbacks. It's just straight down, and when you start down (you can't drive up), you can't see where you're headed. Your Mom or Dad will want to take it slow. Before the zigzag road was built, Lombard Street was even steeper.

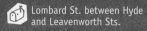

Lombard St. between Hyde and Leavenworth Sts.

Free

Daily 24 hrs

415/974–6900

4 and up

Once you've completed the driving portion, you may want to find a nearby parking space (admittedly easier said than done) to get a more leisurely view as a pedestrian. You can walk straight up or down the Crookedest Street—steps line either side of it—or just position yourself at the top or bottom for a view of the procession of cars. If your kids have their own cameras, they'll no doubt want to join the picture-taking.

Designed with hairpin curves in the 1920s to enable drivers to negotiate the 40% grade, this block of Lombard is beautifully landscaped with flowers, shrubs, and other plants and lined on either side with houses, whose occupants must feel they're living in a fishbowl without the water. Though your visit will add to this feeling, you can take comfort in the knowledge that they must have known what they were in for when they bought the property. After all, they no doubt drove the Crookedest Street themselves.

KEEP IN MIND Don't try this drive with an RV or any extra-long vehicle. If you don't have a car, you can ride a Powell-Hyde cable car to Lombard Street (ask the conductor to call out the nearest stop), and enjoy the scene as a pedestrian.

EATS FOR KIDS **Caffè Sapore** (790 Lombard St., tel. 415/474–1222), a few blocks down the hill, serves up hot and cold sandwiches, salads, soups, and pastries, and you can sit outdoors on nice days. **Zarzuela** (2000 Hyde St., tel. 415/346–0800), a white-tablecloth restaurant two blocks from the Crookedest Street, serves some of the city's best tapas (Spanish-style appetizer plates). The portions are perfect for kids, and service is friendly. **Swensen's Ice Cream** (1999 Hyde St., tel. 415/775–6818), across from Zarzuela, is the place to stop for an ice-cream cone, dispensing dozens of flavors daily.

MAKE*A*CIRCUS

Ladies and gentlemen, boys and girls, step right up. You, too, can be a circus star, thanks to the amazing, death-defying Make*A*Circus—well, okay, maybe not death-defying, but certainly entertaining. This San Francisco–based nonprofit group has been presenting free circus festivals in public parks, recreation centers, school yards, and other outdoor spaces every summer since 1974. As each three-part, three-hour show unfolds, children get to watch a one-ring circus, learn how to perform, and then take the stage themselves.

First comes a fast-paced production of original circus theater, staged by the performers of Make*A*Circus. These musical plays last just under an hour and typically include daring aerial and acrobatic stunts, juggling, clowns, and jazzy music. Next, in a series of half-hour circus-arts workshops, audience members from toddlers to teens are invited to learn some basics of clowning, juggling, tumbling, and building human pyramids. All kids are welcome. There's even a workshop for children under 5, who learn dance and song. The 30- to 60-minute grand finale, which presents the conclusion to the unfinished show,

EATS FOR KIDS Except for a few special shows, such as the opening day performance, Make*A*Circus does not have food concessions, so bring some snacks. After all, what would a circus be without popcorn or peanuts? For restaurants, see listings of attractions nearest the Make*A*Circus performance you attend.

HEY, KIDS! Circuses have been around for thousands of years, but early ones in ancient Rome were quite different from those today. Rome's Circus Maximus could seat 350,000 spectators, who came to watch games, horse-and-chariot races, and fights between gladiators. All of them (not just the fights) could get bloody. Modern-day circuses began about 200 years ago, starting with riders performing tricks on horses in a ring. Later came all the other animals, acrobats, and clowns that we know as part of the traveling tent shows and "big tops."

lets those same kids show off their new skills for their families, friends, and the rest of the audience, who get to whoop and holler with delight at the high-energy antics.

Each summer's show has a theme, often combining fantasy and fable with easy-to-absorb messages about social issues, such as racial intolerance or the dangers of second-hand smoke. In one production, kids became superheroes, traveling down a giant windpipe into a pair of lungs, where they battled the smoke demons, Tar and Nicotine. Meanwhile, a trapeze artist played a pumping heart. The story lines aren't preachy, though; they're too much fun for that.

Besides various San Francisco locations, look for Make∗A∗Circus performances in other Bay Area communities, such as Oakland, Berkeley, San Rafael, and San Jose. Call or check the Web site for a schedule. And then run off to join the circus—at least for a few hours.

KEEP IN MIND If your kids have an itch to perform beyond the circus stage, they might be interested in joining San Francisco–based theater troupes, such as the Young Performers Theatre (Bldg. C, Ft. Mason, tel. 415/ 346–5550), Musical Theater Works (2340 Jackson St., tel. 415/641–5988), ACT Young Conservatory (30 Grant Ave., tel. 415/834–3200 ext. 4), and the Marsh (1062 Valencia St., tel. 415/826–5750 ext. 4). All four groups feature children as stars in their productions, and, best of all, you can watch them perform. Tuition varies by group.

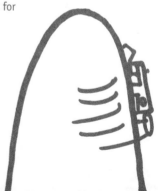

MARINA GREEN

The Marina Green is one of San Francisco's prettiest parks, occupying a prime location along San Francisco Bay. Running the equivalent of eight city blocks, it's a wide stretch of grass and adjacent walkways popular with kite-flyers, runners, in-line skaters, bicyclists, jugglers, sunbathers, picnickers, and touch-football and volleyball players. It's a short walk from the beach at Crissy Field, which is part of the Presidio (see #16), and borders the Marina Small Craft Harbor, where hundreds of pleasure boats are docked. Its western end is across from one of the country's top family museums, the Exploratorium (see #45). If you're walking the gorgeous 3½-mile Golden Gate Promenade, a paved trail that runs from Aquatic Park to the Golden Gate Bridge, you'll pass by here. Wherever you're heading, linger awhile; benches look out toward Alcatraz and the Golden Gate Bridge, and there's plenty of grass for stretching out.

This is one of San Francisco's top spots for kite-flying. On weekends you may see dozens of colorful, elaborate kites—some shaped like dragons, butterflies, or other exotic

KEEP IN MIND Just east of the Marina Green sits Ft. Mason Center (tel. 415/441–3400; www.ftmason.org), a former military post that's now a cultural center containing the Young Performers Theatre (tel. 415/346–5550), where kids are the stars; the Children's Art Center (tel. 415/771–0292), which holds open art classes Monday–Saturday for kids 2–10; offices of the Golden Gate National Recreation Area (tel. 415/556–0560); and some small museums, including the Museo Italo Americano (tel. 415/673–2200) and the San Francisco Craft and Folk Art Museum (tel. 415/775–0990). All are in Building C except the latter, which is in Building A.

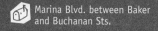

creatures—with long tails flapping in the breezes. Big flat expanses and a regular breeze off the bay usually make flying good for everyone, but occasional tricky winds call for more expert flyers.

With a small detour, you can catch one of San Francisco's most unusual—and overlooked—attractions, at the eastern tip of the breakwater that forms the Marina Small Craft Harbor. Start on the western end of the Marina Green (at the foot of Baker Street); then follow the path past the St. Francis Yacht Club east to the Wave Organ. Here "natural music" is made by waves as they funnel through some 20 granite pipes. Come at high tide for the best effect. Your kids can climb on the rocks while you relax on the stone steps and enjoy the "concert" along with views of yachts and the bay. Even if this is as close as you'll ever get to a yacht, it's a million-dollar experience.

EATS FOR KIDS
Greens to Go (Ft. Mason Center, Bldg. A, tel. 415/771–6330) is a take-out stand at **Greens** vegetarian restaurant (see #4), where you can get sandwiches, salads, and baked goods for picnicking at Marina Green. **Café Marimba** (see #45) has excellent Mexican food.

HEY, KIDS! From Marina Green, face south (away from the water) and look toward the neatly kept houses lining Marina Boulevard. Imagine that you're standing here in October 1989, when a powerful earthquake severely damaged the Marina District. Many houses, streets, and sidewalks crumbled from the enormous waves of energy that traveled all the way from Santa Cruz, 75 miles south. The area is built on landfill—mostly sand. If you've ever built a sand castle, you know how unsteady sand can be.

MARIN HEADLANDS

Just across the Golden Gate Bridge from San Francisco, the Marin Headlands occupy 12,000 acres of rolling coastal hills from East Ft. Baker to the rocky Pacific shores. They're part of the vast Golden Gate National Recreation Area and perhaps best known for their panoramas of the San Francisco skyline as seen through the bridge's soaring orange cables.

The headlands contain more than 100 miles of paved roads, unpaved fire roads, and foot, mountain-bike, and horse trails, but most people's introduction is via scenic Conzelman Road. Accessible from the northern end of the bridge, Conzelman Road hugs the cliffs for 5 miles to Point Bonita, where a ½-mile hike leads to the 1855 Point Bonita Lighthouse, still in operation.

Along the way, you may want to stop and explore some old military fortifications and gun batteries. The tunnels and bunkers, which date from the 1870s, were constructed to help guard the Golden Gate from foreign attack. Battery 129, at Hawk Hill along Conzelman

EATS FOR KIDS There are no restaurants in the Marin Headlands, so bring a picnic lunch and find a hillside or beach with a view. For restaurants in nearby Sausalito, such as **Hamburgers** and **Scoma's**, see #62 and #60.

KEEP IN MIND Ft. Barry's onetime chapel has been converted to the Marin Headlands Visitor Center, which has displays on natural history and serves as the starting point for ranger-led walks. If you're interested in doing some camping or hiking here, call the visitor center or the Golden Gate National Recreation Area for information, directions, and trail conditions. One nice hike is the Tennessee Valley Trail, a relatively flat, 4-mile round-trip from the Tennessee Valley Road parking area to Tennessee Beach on the Pacific. With older kids, you could also try the 8-mile, round-trip hike to Muir Beach.

Road, provides unobstructed 360° views of the bridge, the city, and the bay. Kids often enjoy exploring its tunnels, originally designed for cannons. (Bring flashlights and old clothes.) Many of the old forts have been put to peaceful uses. Ft. Baker, at the foot of the bridge, now houses the Bay Area Discovery Museum (*see* #62).

Several miles west, just above the beach at Ft. Cronkhite, is the Marine Mammal Center (tel. 415/289–7325), open daily 10–4 and free. This rescue and rehab center for sick, injured, or orphaned sea lions, seals, sea otters, whales, and porpoises is one of the world's largest wildlife hospitals. Here you can learn about ocean life, hear how marine biologists rescue whales stranded on nearby beaches, and actually see some recuperating animals, perhaps seal pups being bottle-fed by volunteers. Not far beyond, Rodeo Lagoon is populated with loons, grebes, and other birds. Rodeo Beach lies just past the lagoon. It all adds up to a lot of natural beauty in this part of San Francisco's backyard.

HEY, KIDS! Back in the 1950s and '60s, 300 Nike missile batteries guarded cities and military bases around the United States. The only missile site that's been preserved as it was then is at Ft. Barry, in the Marin Head-lands. Called Nike Missile Site SF88L, it once had 20 missiles ready to shoot down any enemy planes headed toward San Francisco. Fortunately, no mis-sile ever had to be fired. You can tour the site the first Sunday afternoon of each month from 12:30 to 3:30. Your Mom or Dad can call the visitor center for more information.

MISSION CLIFFS

To get your family psyched for tackling the granite cliffs or massive boulders of Yosemite—or at least that big rock in your backyard—head to San Francisco's only indoor rock-climbing gym, one of the largest in the Bay Area. Within a giant former warehouse in the Mission District, Mission Cliffs offers 14,000 square feet of artificial climbing terrain with a 50-foot-high lead wall and 2,000 square feet of bouldering "landscape."

Kids climb brown walls studded with foot and hand holds and are secured by harness and rope to the ceiling or the top of the wall. Your kids can come just to watch, and if they like what they see, they can sign up for classes, offered when instructors are available. Though there's no minimum age, make sure your children are physically and psychologically ready for the experience.

Kids can take private lessons ($35 an hour) with one-on-one instruction; if your child brings a sibling or friend along, the second one receives a discount. Another popular offering is

HEY, KIDS! If you start climbing, you'll want to learn some lingo. "Chickenheads" are large rock formations that offer good hand and foot holds. A "crimper" is a small, painful hold you can only grasp with the tips of your fingers. The "Elvis syndrome" occurs when your leg starts shaking and you can't stop it. (Your parents will understand this one.) A "free solo" is when you climb a rock face without using any kind of "pro" (protection), such as ropes or anchors. Sorry, though, they won't let you try free solos at Mission Cliffs.

 2295 Harrison St.

 415/550-0515;
www.mission-cliffs.com

 $10–$30 adults,
$35 children 4–17;
equipment rentals $5

 M–F 6:30 AM–10 PM, Sa–Su 10–6

4 and up

group birthday parties, which include two hours of supervised climbing for up to 5 kids ($100). Weekly summer camps are offered, too. Instruction not only teaches your children about climbing but also should help them develop balance, coordination, concentration, and self-confidence. Though the atmosphere is informal and fun, supervision is close. Meanwhile, you can watch and relax or learn how to belay your child yourself by taking a Belay Safety Class ("belay" means securing the rope for a rock climber). Recommended for first-time climbers, this class demonstrates the proper use of belay equipment, knot tying, and basic top-rope climbing. Memberships provide discounts on lessons.

With lessons under their harness, most children learn the basics quickly. Many 7–9 year-olds grasp within a week how to put on a harness, tie a knot, belay, and climb. Younger kids generally take longer, but those 10 and up often learn in a lesson or two—perhaps faster than their parents.

KEEP IN MIND

Rock climbing does pose physical risk, and everyone participating must sign a release of liability and assumption of risk form (a parent must sign for kids). If you want to belay your own child, you must first pass a staff-administered test.

EATS FOR KIDS **La Taqueria** (2889 Mission St., tel. 415/285–7117) serves up terrific burritos, tacos, and fresh fruit drinks amid clean, colorful surroundings. The **St. Francis Fountain and Candy Store** (2801 24th St., tel. 415/826–4200), the city's oldest (1918) and most atmospheric soda fountain, is famous for its ice-cream treats and candy, but also offers basic lunches and dinners. For other Mission District eateries, such as **La Cumbre Taqueria**, **Ti Couz**, and **Roosevelt Tamale Parlor**, see #27 and #24.

MISSION DOLORES

Historic buildings may not top your kids' list of "fun things to do," but Mission Dolores has some things going for it. For starters, you can tell them it's the oldest building in San Francisco—more than 200 years old, in fact. The mission was completed in 1791, one of a string of 21 Spanish missions in California founded by Father Junipero Serra around the time the United States was gaining independence from England back on the East Coast.

Don't mistake the humble historic mission for the newer (1913), multidomed basilica next door, where most local parishioners come to worship. The old mission is small—the simplest, by design, of the state's historic missions. It's also one of the best preserved. Be sure your kids look up at the ceiling, where local Costanoans hand-painted Native American designs with vegetable dyes. The tiny chapel is decorated with frescoes and a hand-painted wooden altar; some artifacts were brought from Mexico by mule in the late 18th century. A small museum holds other historic pieces. You can rent an audio tour, which contains interesting background information, but it lasts 45 minutes, so it's best suited for older kids.

KEEP IN MIND For the young and the restless, Mission Dolores Park (18th and Dolores Sts.) is two blocks away. Here you'll find lots of green grass for picnicking and sunbathing, tennis and basketball courts, a playground, a dog-run area, and some great views of the city from its hillsides.

HEY, KIDS! To get to be the oldest building in San Francisco, Mission Dolores has had to manage to keep standing through more than two centuries and three major earthquakes, including the huge 1906 quake and fire that almost wiped out the city. How could it have survived all that shaking and baking when many newer buildings didn't? One reason is that its walls, made of sun-dried adobe, were built 4 feet thick. Those early Spanish settlers really knew how to build things to last.

The old cemetery next to the chapel is the most intriguing sight. Here in the oldest tombs in the city, dozens of early San Francisco pioneers and settlers are buried, including a number of children who died during the Gold Rush days—a poignant reminder of the hardships of those times. Lying in unmarked graves in back are the remains of an estimated 5,000 Native Americans. The cemetery also contains the burial sites of Don Francisco de Haro, the first mayor of San Francisco, and Don Luis Antonio Arguello, the first governor of Alta (or "upper") California, back in the days before California was part of the United States. But it was made famous by a scene in the 1958 Hitchcock film *Vertigo,* in which Kim Novak's character paid a visit here. It's still worth making a trip.

EATS FOR KIDS Picnic at Mission Dolores Park, or choose one of the area's inexpensive ethnic restaurants. **La Cumbre Taqueria** (515 Valencia St., tel. 415/863–8205) has some of the best burritos in the city, and the *carne asada* (grilled steak) is tops. The area can get a little dicey at night, however. **Ti Couz** (3108 16th St., tel. 415/252–7373) specializes in Breton-style crepes, both savory (salmon, mushroom) and sweet (chocolate or fruit filled). Frequent lines at both restaurants, reflecting their popularity, are a potential downside.

MT. TAMALPAIS STATE PARK

Usually called Mt. Tam, Mt. Tamalpais dominates the skyline in Marin County (rising to 2,571 feet) and is the top hiking and mountain biking spot in the Bay Area. Dozens of trails lead to redwoods, waterfalls, and panoramic views stretching to San Francisco, Marin County, the bay, and the Pacific Ocean. About 50 of Mt. Tam's 200 miles of trails are within the 6,300-acre Mt. Tamalpais State Park, which occupies much of the mountain's western and southern slopes. Much of the rest of Mt. Tam lies within the boundaries of the Marin Municipal Water District and the Golden Gate National Recreation Area, including Muir Woods National Monument (*see* #25).

The top hike with young kids is the short, easy Verna Dunshee Trail, which loops around East Peak, the highest of Mt. Tam's three peaks. (The steep Plankwalk Trail then climbs ¼ mile to the top.) Another easy hike, the Mountain Theater Trail, leads from the Rock Spring parking area to a picnic area just below the Mountain Theater, where you can watch stage shows on weekends in May and June; tickets go quickly. With energetic kids ages 10 and

HEY, KIDS! If you like to ride bikes, you might be interested to know that mountain bikes were invented in the valleys below Mt. Tam in the early 1970s and first tested on the mountain. Before that, however, the Mill Valley and Mount Tamalpais Scenic Railway (1896–1930)—the "world's crookedest railroad"—ran up and down Mt. Tam's southern slope, chugging up 281 hairpin curves for 8 miles between downtown Mill Valley and the East Peak summit. Today, you can bike or hike the Old Railroad Grade, but be warned: It's steep! Try it downhill.

801 Panoramic Hwy. (off U.S. 101
north via Hwy. 1), Mill Valley

 Free

Daily 24 hrs

415/388-2070, 800/444-7275 camping
reservations; cal-parks.ca.gov/north/marin/mtsp

4 and up

up, consider expanding your hiking to the redwood-lined Steep Ravine Trail, which drops 1,100 feet; the grueling Dipsea Trail, 6.8 miles one way, site of a famous annual footrace; or the Matt Davis Trail, 6.7 miles one way, which leads across the mountain toward Stinson Beach, a favorite Bay Area spot for sun and surf. Mountain bikes aren't permitted on foot trails, but they are allowed on fire roads, paved roads, and "grades."

Mt. Tam has two campgrounds, Pantoll and Steep Ravine. The Pantoll Campground lies between the mountain summit and Muir Woods and has 16 walk-in tent sites ($7 per night), awarded at the Pantoll ranger station on a first-come, first-served basis. The Steep Ravine Environmental Campground, on an ocean bluff south of Stinson Beach, has 10 rustic cabins ($15 a night) and six tent sites ($7). Parking permits and reservations are required year-round.

EATS FOR KIDS
Picnic tables are available at Rock Spring, Bootjack, Laurel Dell Meadow, and the East Peak summit, which also has a **snack bar**. The **Mountain Home Inn** (810 Panoramic Hwy., tel. 415/381-9000) serves breakfast weekends, lunch and dinner Tuesday–Sunday. The **Buckeye Roadhouse** (15 Shoreline Hwy., tel. 415/331-2600) has classic American fare.

KEEP IN MIND Weather can play a big role in your enjoyment of Mt. Tam and may vary widely on the mountain itself: It's easy to go from warm sun into cool fog. The southern and western slopes, especially, are often fog-covered from June through August, and the best chance for clear skies and views is in late spring and fall, though winter also produces its share of crystal-clear days. Most rain falls between November and April. Spring wildflower season is at its peak from March until mid-May, and yellow jackets may plague picnic areas in summer.

MUIR WOODS NATIONAL MONUMENT

Snuggled in a cool, often foggy redwood-lined canyon on the southeastern lower slopes of Mt. Tamalpais, just 12 miles north of the Golden Gate Bridge, Muir Woods National Monument is the world's most famous stand of old-growth redwoods—the last remnants of soaring trees that once covered the mountain and many parts of the Bay Area. As California's most-visited redwood park (more than 1 million visitors a year), this is definitely nature for the masses: The main hiking trails are paved, and the woods are a regular stop on tour bus excursions. But the virgin redwoods—accented with green ferns and colorful azaleas, the scents of moss and bay, and the sounds of splashing Redwood Creek—are so majestic that tranquility still seems to prevail.

You won't find the tallest redwoods here—those are farther north—but the trees in Muir Woods are up to 250 feet tall. Many were already growing in the days of the Crusades.

Six miles of trails lie fully within the 560-acre park, and several can be negotiated by

EATS FOR KIDS A **café** near the main entrance serves burgers, hot dogs, and apple pie. Picnicking isn't permitted in Muir Woods but is allowed in nearby Muir Beach and adjacent Mt. Tamalpais State Park. See the latter for information on picnicking and area restaurants.

KEEP IN MIND A few tips can help avoid disappointment or discomfort while visiting Muir Woods: Arrive by midmorning or in late afternoon to avoid the crush of visitors, and go midweek if possible. (Parking lots, including the overflow lots, often fill up.) Roads to the park are steep and winding, and long trailers are prohibited. Bring jackets or sweatshirts; redwoods flourish in cool, foggy climates, and this is one of them. Watch for poison oak and stinging nettles just off the trails. Better yet, stay on the trails. Although camping isn't permitted here, you can camp in adjacent Mt. Tamalpais State Park.

kids of just about any age. The 2 miles of paved trails along the canyon floor are mostly level and suited for strollers, and four bridges spanning Redwood Creek allow you to make short loops. The tallest trees in the park are found along the Main Trail in Bohemian Grove (a ½-mile loop from the parking lot) and in Cathedral Grove (a 1-mile loop). With school-aged kids, venture just a bit farther, along the unpaved trails—such as the Ben Johnson Trail (2½ miles round-trip)—that lead up out of the canyon into Mt. Tamalpais State Park (*see* #26), and you'll be surprised at how few other folks you'll meet.

If your kids are ages 6–12, they might want to join the park service's Junior Ranger Program here. They'll learn to measure the temperature of the creek and look for creatures such as salmon, deer, and ladybugs. But whatever their age, children will probably spend at least some time just gaping in wonder at the awesome natural giants around them.

HEY, KIDS! Redwood trees like those at Muir Woods are found only along a narrow stretch of the western coast of the United States, from the state of Oregon south to Monterey, California, which is about 120 miles south of San Francisco. Even though the word "sequoia" is part of their scientific name (*Sequoia sempervirens*), these trees are different from the giant sequoias you'd see at Yosemite or Sequoia national parks. Those trees are bigger around but don't grow as tall as the highest redwoods.

MURALS OF THE MISSION DISTRICT

They're some of the city's least-known artistic treasures—possibly more famous in Europe than in San Francisco—and you don't need to visit a museum to see them. All you have to do is take a walk (or a bike ride or a drive). Hundreds of outdoor murals decorate the Mission District, and their often brilliant colors and bold subjects can captivate kids just as much as adults.

The first—and still best-known—group of murals is in little Balmy Alley (24th to 25th St. between Harrison and Treat Sts.). Back in the early 1970s, community artists—both adults and children, working alone or in groups—started to adorn the block-long byway's walls with murals featuring such themes as peace in Central America, Latino heritage, and neighborhood pride. (The Mission District is heavily Hispanic.) Since then, dozens more muralists have joined in, so that today much of the street, including walls, fences, and garage doors, is covered with artwork.

EATS FOR KIDS Restaurants with a heavy emphasis on Mexican and Latin American food line 24th Street. One, **Roosevelt Tamale Parlor** (2817 24th St., tel. 415/550–9213), has been dishing up Tex-Mex classics since 1922. **La Victoria Mexican Bakery** (2937 24th St., tel. 415/550–9292), where you can buy Mexican-style pastries, is another long-time favorite, as is the **St. Francis Fountain and Candy Store** (*see* #28). For information on other eating places in the Mission District, such as **La Cumbre Taqueria** and **Ti Couz**, which specializes in crepes, see #27.

Like those in Balmy Alley, most Mission District murals are in the area bordered on the west by Mission Street, the east by Potrero Avenue, the north by 20th Street, and the south by Precita Avenue, next to Precita Park. Down the block from Balmy Alley, Precita Eyes Mural Arts and Visitors Center sells Mission mural walk maps for $1.50, allowing you to take your own self-guided tour any time you like.

You can also take a guided walking tour. They are best for children 10 and older who are particularly interested in art, but all ages are welcome. Use your best judgment. Precita Eyes offers the most frequent walking tours, which last 1½–2 hours and cover a six- to eight-block area with 75–90 murals. Drop-in tours are given on weekends; call for reservations for other days. A ½-hour slide show on the making of murals precedes the afternoon tour. Tour guides—muralists themselves—are attuned to the needs of kids. For any walk, whether guided or self guided, wear comfortable shoes, and carry snacks and water.

KEEP IN MIND
In addition to the tours conducted through the Precita Eyes Mural Arts and Visitors Center, less frequent—but free—walking tours of the Mission murals are offered by City Guides (tel. 415/557–4266). These tours are given only on selected Saturdays, so call for a schedule.

HEY, KIDS! Though it's hard to pick out specific murals among all those in Balmy Alley, look for one called "Indigenous Eyes: War and Peace." (It's on a garage door about halfway down the alley.) And yes, the skeleton and dove in each eye stand for war and peace. It depicts life in Central America during years of civil war and unrest. Another colorful mural shows a San Francisco bus, tropical birds, monkeys, and little children. What do you think it's trying to say?

NOB HILL

Nob Hill, which rises steeply to a height of 376 feet above Chinatown and the Financial District, has been one of the city's most prestigious addresses since the late 19th century, when railroad magnates and Comstock Lode silver barons built the most expensive homes California had ever seen here. All but one of the houses were destroyed in the 1906 earthquake, and the lone survivor, the brownstone Flood Mansion, is now the exclusive Pacific Union Club. But the legacy of the "Big Four" railroad magnates—Charles Crocker, Mark Hopkins, Collis P. Huntington, and Leland Stanford—and other tycoons lives on in the luxury apartment buildings and hotels (including the Mark Hopkins, Huntington, and Fairmont) that line this high-rent hill.

To rub elbows with the wealthy—or, at least, their dogs, kids, and nannies—take a break at the top of the hill in neat, tidy Huntington Park. Find a spot on a bench while your kids take to the swings, slide, and climbing structures on the sand-based playground. This is a dog-friendly park. Chances are at least one pooch will be chasing a Frisbee

EATS FOR KIDS The **Nob Hill Café** (1152 Taylor St., tel. 415/776–6500) dishes up pastas, pizza, and chocolaty desserts in friendly surroundings. Don't confuse it with the **Nob Hill Noshery Café** (1400 Pacific Ave., tel. 415/928–6674), which serves three meals a day. Best bets are the deli-style sandwiches.

HEY, KIDS! Wonder how Nob Hill got its name? Nob came from "nabob," a term used in colonial India for a man of wealth or importance. Once, the area was simply called California Street Hill. In 1873 the arrival of the cable car made it easier to scale the hill from the Financial District. As a result, many of the richest San Franciscans—the local "nabobs"—moved up here, and a new nickname was coined. To this day, Nob Hill is still one of the wealthiest neighborhoods in the city.

while others are chasing each other (not in the children's play area, however). Watch for expensive pedigrees; after all, this *is* Nob Hill.

The park sits across from Grace Cathedral (Taylor and California Sts.), modeled after Notre Dame in Paris. The Episcopal cathedral has a 15th-century French altarpiece, luminous stained-glass windows, and gilded-bronze doors similar to Filippo Brunelleschi's Baptistery doors in Florence, Italy. So visiting here is like taking the kids on a mini-trip to Europe. Don't overlook the cathedral's intriguing indoor and outdoor labyrinths, based on one at France's Chartres Cathedral. Each labyrinth forms a meandering path that leads in a geometric pattern to the center of a circle and back out again, representing an interfaith path of prayer and meditation. Though many children like to walk the labyrinths, they should respect others following the paths and not use them for racing. Fortunately, the park is nearby for restless kids—and there's always a hill for them to climb, too.

KEEP IN MIND Part of the fun of visiting Nob Hill is riding the California Street cable car line to the top. The ride is steep and as much fun as many theme park rides for kids. You can board the cable car anywhere along California Street between Van Ness Avenue and the foot of Market Street. Rides cost $2 each for anyone 6 or older; little ones are free. For more about riding cable cars, see #58. If you do decide to drive, note that street parking is tight, and parking garages are expensive.

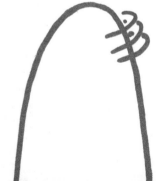

OAKLAND MUSEUM OF CALIFORNIA

Maybe because it's across San Francisco Bay in Oakland, this attractive, innovative museum on the south shore of Lake Merritt (*see* #52 for lake activities) doesn't get the recognition it deserves. Its architecture alone—three tiers of galleries with gardens, courts, terraces, lawns, and pond in a complex covering four square blocks—makes it stand out. But if you want to get a sense of California's history, environment, art, and diversity all in one place, the Oakland Museum is a must.

In the Cowell Hall of California History, your kids can whisk their imaginations back to the days of Native Americans, missions and ranchos, the Gold Rush, the Victorian era, and 1960s-era California—captured in the film *American Graffiti* and in the spirit of San Francisco's Summer of Love—right up to the current technology of Silicon Valley. The Hall of California Ecology is the museum's other top family spot. Here you and your children can take a simulated walk across the state—from the coast to the Sierra Nevada to the desert—to view the terrain, vegetation, and wildlife as it looked before the arrival of Europeans. In the Aquatic

KEEP IN MIND Oakland has another kid-friendly museum that's less known but well worth a visit: the Museum of Children's Art (538 9th St., tel. 510/465–8770), known as MOCHA. The two-floor museum displays art created by children, ranging from East Bay kids to those who live in other countries. MOCHA also has plenty of art supplies on hand, so kids can produce their own masterpieces. Classes and camps are offered as well. The museum is free, and it's open Tuesday–Saturday 10–6 and Sunday 12–5.

1000 Oak St., at 10th St., Oakland

 $6 adults, $4 children 6–17 and students; 2nd Su of mth free

 W–Sa 10–5, Su 12–5, 1st F of mth 10–9

510/238–2200; www.museumca.org

6 and up

California Gallery, you can get an overview of the state's ocean, river, stream, and estuary environments. With older kids, you might want to add the Gallery of California Art, where you'll find some 500 paintings, sculptures, prints, photographs, and decorative arts produced by California artists from the early 19th century on. Watch for sketches and paintings by early artist-explorers, Gold Rush genre pictures, colorful landscapes, and more modern Bay Area Pop and works.

The museum offers a variety of special events and workshops for families and kids, on subjects such as photography, dinosaurs, and box making. (Some are free; others require a materials fee.) Major temporary exhibits, covering such different topics as hot-rod culture and California caves, are displayed in the Great Hall, and the museum's courtyards often host open-air art exhibitions. It's enough to lure even die-hard San Franciscans over to the East Bay—an impressive feat in itself.

EATS FOR KIDS
The museum's **OMCA Café** features hot entrées, sandwiches, soups, salads, snacks, and desserts. Another option is to spread out a blanket under the shade trees along the banks of Lake Merritt and have a picnic. Nearby **Zza's Trattoria** (see #52) is a child-friendly Italian restaurant.

HEY, KIDS! In the Cowell Hall of California History, watch for the three interactive History Information Stations: touch-screen computers that give further information about the things you see on display. Some of them have video footage of people telling stories about California history. There's even a game you can play that takes you around the gallery to try to find certain objects. It's a way to have a little fun and learn more about the state's history at the same time.

OAKLAND ZOO

Once known as one of the worst zoos in the country, with cramped and depressing animal enclosures, the Oakland Zoo embarked on a long-term renovation program two decades ago and now has facilities approaching those in some of the state's top zoos. It comprises 50 different exhibits on 100 acres within Knowland Park, harboring nearly 400 native and exotic animals.

Just inside the entrance, you're greeted by bright pink flamingos in Flamingo Plaza, which makes a good orientation or meeting point. Straight ahead of Flamingo Plaza are the monkey, ape, and chimp habitats, perhaps the zoo's most interesting area. On especially lush, tropical Siamang Island and Gibbon Island, hooting primates swing through the trees in a rainforest environment. Head off to the right for the African Veldt and Savanna areas, where giraffes, gazelles, lions, and elephants reside. The African Savanna, which simulates desert areas of eastern and southern Africa, is landscaped with man-made rocks, a waterfall, and Kikuyu-style "mud and cow dung" (actually disguised concrete) structures. The 20

KEEP IN MIND Though the zoo is normally open daily, it closes during bad weather. What's bad enough to make it close? If you're still in doubt after looking out the window, call the park to ask before setting out with your kids and risking disappointment.

EATS FOR KIDS The zoo's **Safari Café,** near the entrance, has standard concession food and some outdoor tables. There's also a **food stand** in the Rides Area. Knowland Park has plenty of grassy picnic areas with tables and barbecue facilities. Though there are no restaurants right near the zoo, you can head for Oakland's family-friendly Lake Merritt area (take I–580 west from the zoo to the Grand Avenue exit), site of **Zza's Trattoria** and **Zachary's Chicago Pizza** (see #52).

9777 Golf Links Rd. (off I–580),
Knowland Park, Oakland

510/632-9525;
www.oaklandzoo.org

 $6.50 ages 15 and up,
$4.50 children 2–14

Daily 10–4

All ages

species that call it home include warthogs, hyenas, green monkeys, and meerkats. Your children may enjoy climbing into a tube for a "meerkat's-eye view" of the savanna.

To the left and rear is the Children's Zoo (free with admission), where your kids can watch river otters, bobcats, pythons, iguanas, and alligators and can pet and feed domestic sheep and pygmy goats. In the Rides Area, near the front, they can board a ⅔-size replica of a Civil War–era locomotive ($1.50). Look for the carousel, too, as well as some small carnival-type rides, but be sure to check the height limits to make sure your kids aren't too big. If they are, they may be ready for the Skyride ($1.50), a chairlift that provides a bird's-eye, 15-minute view of American bison and tule elk in the North American Range area. The open cars go quite high, which might scare young kids. No need for that, though, since there's plenty to see at ground level in this vastly improved zoo.

HEY, KIDS! Chances are when you enter the park's Asian rain-forest area—or probably before—you'll hear lots of hooting and screeching noises. No, that's not a visiting school class. It's the siamangs and gibbons, types of apes from Southeast Asia. Siamangs can be heard as far as 2 miles away! Both siamangs and gibbons use their calling to mark their territory. That means they're telling other monkeys to stay away. Males and females sing different parts, kind of like a very loud—and very screechy—jungle duet.

OCEAN BEACH

San Francisco's best-known beach is a wide, mostly flat, 4-mile blanket of sand that forms the western, Pacific Ocean edge of the city. Overseen by the National Park Service, Ocean Beach stretches south from the Cliff House to Ft. Funston (*see* #49 and #42), which occupy cliffs overlooking it from opposite directions.

On warm, sunny days, the beach is typically packed with sunbathers, Frisbee tossers, dog walkers, and kite-flyers taking advantage of the ocean breezes—and sometimes gusty winds. This is also a favored spot for watching the sunset. Some people never get out of their parked cars. Even on foggy, misty days—and there are many here—Ocean Beach is a gathering place for a diverse group of people in search of recreation. Anglers cast their lines for perch and stripers, and just below the Cliff House, expert surfers ride the waves. (This is not a place for beginners.) Because of the often rough, treacherous surf, swimming is dangerous; currents are unpredictable, the undertow is strong, and there are no lifeguards. Besides, the water is downright cold. Watch kids carefully even if they're just playing along the shore.

EATS FOR KIDS The **Beach Chalet** (1000 Great Hwy., tel. 415/386–8439), an often crowded brew pub, serves up buffalo wings, gumbo, and ocean views across the Great Highway from Ocean Beach. For restaurants in and near the Cliff House, such as **Louis'**, see #49, and for restaurants near the southern sections of Ocean Beach, such as **John's Ocean Beach Cafe,** see #10. Otherwise, just bring your own food and have a picnic on the beach. Beach fires are permitted at times, but check with rangers about regulations beforehand.

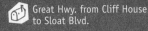 Great Hwy. from Cliff House to Sloat Blvd.

 Free

Daily 24 hrs

415/556-8642;
www.nps.gov/goga/clho/ocbe

All ages

One of the main draws of Ocean Beach runs right alongside it for the first mile or so down from the Cliff House: a broad paved pathway that attracts cyclists, rollerbladers, runners, walkers, and parents pushing strollers. Another pathway runs along the opposite side of the Great Highway, bordering Golden Gate Park, and remains paved all the way to Sloat Boulevard, about 3 miles away, where you can connect with the bike path around Lake Merced (*see* #36). Because you'll ride on the road a bit toward the end, the latter portion of the bike route is suitable for older kids only.

Yet despite all the activity, Ocean Beach remains essentially unspoiled and free of commercial development. No buildings block ocean views; no concessions operate south of the Cliff House. It's a place where both local and visiting families can find fun, in sun or fog.

HEY, KIDS! There used to be a seaside amusement park across from Ocean Beach called Playland at the Beach. It was torn down years ago and replaced by rows of condos. But you can still ride the old Playland carousel—it's now spinning away at Yerba Buena Gardens, downtown.

KEEP IN MIND The western edges of Golden Gate Park (*see* #39) lie just across the highway from Ocean Beach. You can take your kids to see two historic windmills here. One, a restored 1902 Dutch windmill in the northwestern corner of the park, overlooks a tulip garden. The other, called the Murphy Windmill, was the world's largest when it was built in 1905, but has fallen into disrepair. Both once pumped water to the Strawberry Hill reservoir in the middle of the park.

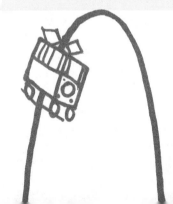

PARAMOUNT'S GREAT AMERICA

Tackling 10 roller coasters and other daredevil rides at this movie- and TV-theme park is nothing less than a rite of passage for many Bay Area youngsters. Ten-year-olds who board the Vortex for a heart-thumping, stand-up roller-coaster ride know they're growing up; 12-year-olds who brave a 22-story, 91-feet-per-second, open-air fall on the Drop Zone can claim bragging rights all winter over those who held back.

Psycho Mouse takes you through 14 twists and hairpin turns. Top Gun, a jet coaster meant to simulate the sensation of flying an F-14 Tomcat jet fighter, provides short but intense thrills. As you catapult off into space at 50 mph, you experience a 360° vertical loop, two 270° "afterburn turns," and a "zero-gravity barrel roll." Another stomach-turner, Invertigo, takes riders forward and backward at 55 mph through a boomerang and vertical loop. The 7th Portal, a 3-D ride, combines computer animation and motion-simulation technology to transport would-be superheroes through cyberspace.

HEY, KIDS!

The 7th Portal, based on the animated on-line series, was created by Stan Lee, a cartoonist who helped create Spider-man, the Incredible Hulk, and the X-Men. He's been inventing superheroes for so long that, chances are, even your parents have heard of him.

KEEP IN MIND A few tips can help you get the most out of your visit. Note that most of the scarier rides have minimum height requirements, and some of the kiddie rides have maximum height requirements (adults must be accompanied by kids). Explaining this to children of borderline height might ward off disappointment. If your kids plan to visit Splat City or go on water rides, bring a change of clothing, or have them wear swimsuits. And if you plan to return soon, ask about free upgrades to WOW! cards, included in the general admission price and good for unlimited repeat visits during the season.

Great America Pkwy. between
U.S. 101 and Hwy. 237, Santa Clara

 408/988–1776; www.pgathrills.com

 $43 ages 7 and up, $33
children 3–6 or under 48"

 Late Mar–mid-Oct, varying days
(early June–late Aug, daily),
10–varying hrs

3 and up

Younger kids gravitate toward Nickelodeon Splat City—a 3-acre tribute to messiness where everyone is guaranteed to get drenched with gallons of water and Green Slime—and the adjacent Kidzville, which has more than 20 rides and attractions. These include a mini–roller coaster, a little parachute drop, and the Kidzville Construction Company play space. The classic double-deck Carousel Columbia, near the park's front entrance, is the world's tallest. Great America also has mid-range rides that are exciting but less scary than Top Gun or Invertigo for squeamish (or should we say reasonable and rational?) youngsters or parents. Among these are the Grizzly, a classic wooden roller coaster, and three water rides, including Rip Roaring Rapids, a rafting ride that's great for getting soaked on a hot day.

For a quieter way to cool off and wind down, the park offers a number of stage shows combining music, cartoon characters, and, in some cases, audience participation. There's also a seven-story IMAX theater. In all, there's plenty to entertain every member of the family—whether fearless or prudent.

EATS FOR KIDS Among park concessions, **Shaggy's Snack Shack,** in Kidzville, has burgers and fries, as does the **American Grill,** a '50s-style diner in Orleans Place. **Wings,** in Yukon Territory, carries rotisserie chicken and chili. The **Pasta Connection** is in Yankee Harbor, and **Maggie Brown's,** in Hometown Square, has chicken dinners. **Food Festival** locations carry an assortment of sandwiches, pizza, hot dogs, and more. The park doesn't allow you to bring any food inside the gates but does provide a picnic area outside the main entrance.

PIER 39

This once-abandoned cargo pier on the eastern edge of Fisherman's Wharf (*see* #43) was transformed into a waterside shopping and entertainment mall in the late 1970s, and it's been San Francisco's top tourist draw ever since. Publicists claim it's the country's most popular non-Disney attraction, and if you go at the height of tourist season, you probably won't dispute it.

Although many San Franciscans consider it a tacky tourist trap, local kids still head here in droves, alongside the out-of-towners. The good news is that it costs nothing to walk in and soak up the atmosphere and the bay views. For those, just follow the wooden boardwalks to the sides or rear of the pier. Rest assured, however: If you leave Pier 39 without lightening your wallet, you'll fall into the vast minority. More than 100 shops—including places to buy toys and candy—as well as eateries and entertainments line the double-deck pier. An antique Venetian carousel entices younger children. Turbo Ride, a motion-simulated adventure ride, is popular with preteens and teens, who also flock to two arcades to test themselves at

EATS FOR KIDS Pier 39 has 11 restaurants and is loaded with snack shops. One of the better ones is **Sea Lion Café** (tel. 415/434–2260), which serves fish-and-chips and overlooks the sea lions. The specialties at the **Boudin Sourdough Bakery & Café** (tel. 415/421–0185) are clam chowder and chili in a bread bowl, great on a cool, foggy day. The **Burger Cafe** (tel. 415/986–5966) has a '50s theme with burgers, fries, and outdoor as well as indoor tables. For information about the **Jail House Cafe,** the **Eagle Café,** and **Bubba Gump Shrimp Co. Restaurant,** see #68 and #65.

video games and bumper cars. A theater shows the special effects–laden *The Great San Francisco Adventure* (tel. 415/956-3456), and the Aquarium of the Bay (*see* #65) sits off to one side. The pier also houses the Blue & Gold Fleet sightseeing ferries (*see* #61) along with a large marina.

Those with slender budgets and iron willpower, however, can spend enjoyable hours here with little cash outlay. Jugglers, magicians, and acrobats perform for loose change. But the best show may be a colony of California sea lions, which took up residence at the West Marina here in 1990 and have been delighting onlookers ever since. Their numbers vary depending on the season (winter is best, summer slimmest), but you may encounter anywhere from dozens to hundreds of the playful pinnipeds, who provide captivating displays of barking, frolicking, and jockeying for sunbathing position on the docks. And they don't even pass the hat at the end—at least, not yet.

HEY, KIDS! If you've ever seen a "trained seal" perform, it probably was really a sea lion. Sea lions and harbor seals look a lot alike, but in fact they aren't closely related. There's an easy way to tell the difference: if it barks, it's a sea lion.

KEEP IN MIND Naturally, the sea lions don't have opening and closing hours, and you can watch them here any day of the week. However, to learn more about them, come for one of the free guided talks, offered on weekends 12–4 by docents from Marin County's Marine Mammal Center (*see* #29). The Marine Mammal Center also runs one of the pier's better stores (tel. 415/289-7373), selling clothing items, books, and gifts, with receipts benefiting that worthy cause.

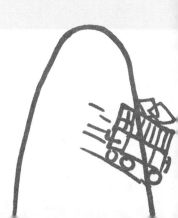

POINT REYES NATIONAL SEASHORE

The Point Reyes peninsula provides 71,000 acres of sheer natural wonder on the Marin County coast. You can hike to secluded beaches or through forests of pine and fir, view wildlife ranging from sea birds to tule elk, and drive through rugged, rolling grasslands. In a region known for its outstanding natural attractions, Point Reyes may top them all.

You could easily spend a day just in the area around the Bear Valley visitor center, the first site you reach after driving up the coast—especially appealing with younger kids. The intriguing, ½-mile-loop Earthquake Trail follows the San Andreas Fault near the epicenter of the famed 1906 San Francisco quake. A nearby ¼-mile trail leads to Kule Lokto, a replica of a Coast Miwok Indian village. At the Morgan Horse Ranch, horses are trained for the National Park Service. The Bear Valley Trail, suited for many kids ages 5 and up, is an easy, 3-mile round-trip through a forest to a meadow and back; with older kids, you can stretch it to an 8-mile round-trip leading to a string of secluded, golden-sand beaches.

EATS FOR KIDS Picnic at any beach. Drakes Beach even has a **snack bar** and picnic tables. Pick up supplies at **Perry's Delicatessen** (Sir Francis Drake Blvd., Inverness Park, tel. 415/663–1491). The **Station House Cafe** (Hwy. 1, Pt. Reyes Station, tel. 415/663–1515) has good sandwiches, salads, and patio dining.

HEY, KIDS! When you walk the Earthquake Trail here, do you feel like the earth is moving? Even when there's no earthquake rumbling along the San Andreas Fault, the land on the west of the fault (the Pacific plate) is moving north past the land east of the fault at the steady rate of 2 inches per year. Even at that snail's pace, the peninsula where you're now standing could eventually end up in Alaska. And if that sounds weird, consider that it once stood in *Southern* California!

Visitor center, Bear Valley Rd., Olema

 415/464–5100, 415/663–8054
camping; www.nps.gov/pore

 Free

 Daily sunrise–sunset (except camping)

3 and up

If you're seeking easier beach access, head for Limantour Spit or Drakes Beach, both on sheltered Drakes Bay, where the water is usually calm but cold. Along a windswept, 15-mile stretch of Pacific Ocean are Point Reyes Beach North and South, where the surf is dangerous but the beachcombing great. In the northern reaches of the park, a 4-mile trail leads to spectacular Tomales Point and frequent sightings of tule elk; this hike is only for older kids with stamina. To reach Point Reyes Light, an 1870 lighthouse perched over the Pacific, you need to drive 22 scenic but winding miles from the Bear Valley visitor center and then climb down 300 steps to the lighthouse, which also means climbing 300 steps back up. On winter weekends, whale-watching is so popular that you may have to park your car down the road and take a shuttle bus to get here.

GETTING THERE Highway 1 up the coast is scenic, but it's also very slow and winding. You can reach Point Reyes from San Francisco in 90 minutes or less by taking U.S. 101 north to the San Anselmo exit. Turn left onto Sir Francis Drake Boulevard and stay on it all the way to the town of Olema. At the stoplight here, turn right onto Highway 1; then take a quick left onto Bear Valley Road, which leads to the visitor center about ½ mile farther north. Pick up a map here to find other park locations.

PRESIDIO NATIONAL PARK

Until fairly recently, this nearly 1,500-acre park overlooking the Golden Gate was a longtime military post. The Spanish came in 1776, establishing a walled fortification (or *presidio*) to protect the bay. After passing into Mexico's hands in 1822, the Presidio fell to the United States when California was acquired in 1846; it became the Sixth Army's base and a training ground for Civil War soldiers. In 1994, the Army moved out, and the Presidio became part of the Golden Gate National Recreation Area. Full conversion to recreational and other uses is a long-term and sometimes controversial process, but already the Presidio contains miles of bike routes and hiking trails that wind along coastal bluffs, past hundreds of historic military buildings and defense installations, and over hills thick with cypress, eucalyptus, and pine trees. Hikers and cyclists get dazzling views of the bay, the Golden Gate Bridge, and the Marin Headlands.

You can soak up some Presidio history at Ft. Point National Historic Site (*see* #41) and at the Presidio Army Museum. The latter contains uniforms, maps, weapons, and displays on

KEEP IN MIND There's so much to see and do in the Presidio that it's hard to know where to start, and winding roads can make finding certain locations a bit tricky. So stop in at the Presidio Visitors Information Center, which has maps, brochures, trail guides, and schedules for free, ranger-led guided walks and bike tours. The latter are best suited for kids ages 10 and up. On weekends, the ranger walks last from 45 minutes to three hours and cover the Presidio's natural history, the area's strategic military history, and the bay-side tidal zone.

Main gate, Lombard and Lyon Sts.; visitor center, Lincoln Blvd. and Montgomery St.

 Free

 Visitor center daily 9–5, museum W–Su 12–4

 415/561–4323 visitor center, 415/556–0560 park service; www.nps.gov/prsf

All ages

the 1906 San Francisco earthquake and the 1915 Panama-Pacific Exposition. Outside is a pair of green cottages that homeless survivors of the 1906 quake rented for $2 a month.

At Crissy Field, which was redeveloped in 2001 into a parklike area along the bay east of the Golden Gate Bridge, you can wade at a beach, watch windsurfers in the bay or birds in a tidal marsh, picnic, bike, skate, or fly kites. Baker Beach, a scenic stretch of sand west of the bridge, is popular for sunbathing but has dangerous surf. The Presidio Golf Course and nearby Julius Kahn playground—with basketball and tennis courts, a softball field, and grass for picnics—are in the park's southern reaches. Mountain Lake Park, also on its southern flanks, has a bi-level playground overlooking a pretty lake. The Presidio Bowling Center completes an array of onetime military recreational facilities now open to the public. And it's all just steps away from many San Francisco homes.

EATS FOR KIDS
The Presidio's picnic areas include tables at Crissy Field and barbecue facilities behind Baker Beach. For information about the Presidio's **Burger King** with a view, see #41, and for other nearby restaurants, see #56 and #45.

HEY, KIDS! One place to visit in the park is the Presidio Pet Cemetery, where military families buried their furry loved ones. It's surrounded by a picket fence, but you can walk in and stop to look at the pictures, poems, and sweet messages that owners attached to their pets' gravestones. The cemetery is a little hard to find, so ask your Mom or Dad to get directions from the visitor center. Not far away, soldiers are buried in the National Cemetery.

RANDALL MUSEUM

This small children's museum run by the city's Recreation and Park Department is so far off the beaten path that it's a wonder anyone ever finds it. Yet savvy San Francisco parents know that its value far outweighs its size and out-of-the-way location. Set in Corona Heights Park, the Randall occupies a dramatic perch overlooking the city between the Haight-Ashbury and Castro districts. Inside, the museum is chock-full of intriguing hands-on exhibits in the realms of nature, art, and science.

Your children will find minerals to touch, dinosaur bones to peruse, and chemistry and biology labs to test out. An earthquake exhibit has a working seismograph, a demonstration of how the earth's shifting tectonic plates can cause quakes, and a fun area called Make-a-Quake, in which kids get to jump up and down to see how much "seismic force" they can produce themselves. Probably the museum's most popular feature, though, is its live animal room, where your children can learn about and get close-up looks at more than 100 critters, such as owls, snakes, mice, and raccoons, that have been injured or were kept as pets

GETTING THERE From Haight Street, go south on Masonic Avenue (away from the Golden Gate Park panhandle) and over the hill. The last block of Masonic winds left down the hill one block onto Roosevelt Way. Turn left on Roosevelt, then right on Museum Way to the parking lot.

KEEP IN MIND Corona Heights Park (sometimes called Museum Hill or Red Rock) offers one of the great "hidden" overlooks of San Francisco. The views are a real bonus, especially for parents, but older kids often enjoy following the trails and the steep climb to the top of the rocks. The lure for young kids is a park and playground with swings and sand, and there are tennis and basketball courts, too. For these last three activities, follow paths down the hill from the museum.

and can no longer live in the wild. Young kids especially take to the petting corral, where they can stroke rabbits and ducks. Staff members give free animal talks on Saturdays.

The museum has put together a strong program for families. Year-round, the Randall offers nature and art classes for all ages (registration required) that last 8–10 weeks for one hour per week. Art classes might include woodworking, ceramics, and jewelry making; nature classes might focus on biology or the environment. The Randall also hosts drop-in Saturday workshops for families that feature a variety of hands-on activities, stages seasonal events such as Halloween parties, and sponsors scheduled field trips, such as hikes to see migrating geese. The Randall Theatre has concerts, films, and performances. Pick up a schedule at the museum for details. But just about anytime, you can count on lots of activity at this little treasure.

EATS FOR KIDS There are no eating places in the immediate vicinity of the museum, so plan to either bring picnic food to Corona Heights Park or search out restaurants in adjoining neighborhoods. If you approach the Randall from the Haight-Ashbury district, try **Sweet Heat** (1725 Haight St., tel. 415/387–8845), where you can pick up inexpensive tacos and burritos. A few blocks east down the hill from the museum in the Castro District, **Sparky's Diner** (242 Church St., tel. 415/621–6001) serves diner-style breakfasts as well as burgers and fries.

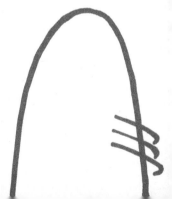

SAN FRANCISCO BAY NATIONAL WILDLIFE REFUGE

Lying just north of San Jose on the southern reaches of San Francisco Bay, this was the country's first urban wildlife refuge, founded in 1972, and it's still one of the most popular—both with wildlife and humans. With 43,000 protected acres along 25 miles of shoreline, the refuge has an extensive system of boardwalks and trails for hiking and cycling, from which you can view potentially hundreds of wildlife species in the salt ponds, marshes, and mudflats. During fall and spring migrations, it's a way station for more than a million shorebirds, waterfowl, and wading birds: sandpipers, peregrine falcons, snowy egrets, great blue herons, canvasback ducks, mallards, kites, terns, and brown pelicans. Harbor seals also often hang around.

Administered by the U.S. Fish and Wildlife Service, the refuge is part of a large complex of U.S.-run refuges in the Bay Area, including the Farallon National Wildlife Refuge (*see* #44). Stop at the visitor center to see exhibits, use the observation deck, and pick up trail information. Several trailheads are nearby. The best for kids is the Tidelands Trail, which

HEY, KIDS! While at the wildlife refuge, you might see lots of birds along with lizards, snakes, rabbits, and other small animals (a pair of binoculars could help). But if you'd come here 200 years ago, you might have seen tule elk, salmon—even grizzly bears! What was once a land of plenty, someone wrote, is now "a land of plenty buildings and roads." In fact, as you stand on the observation deck near the visitor center, you can watch cars whizzing past on the Dumbarton Bridge. But amid the traffic, many forms of wildlife still find a refuge here.

Visitor center, 1 Marshlands Rd., Fremont; education center, 1751 Grand Blvd., Alviso

 510/792-0222 visitor center, 408/262-5513 education center; desfbay.fws.gov

 Free

Daily sunrise–sunset, visitor center T–Su 10–5, education center Sa–Su 10–5

 6 and up

meanders up and down a hill, along the shoreline, and across footbridges for 1⅓ miles. A dozen more miles of trails, as well as more displays and an observation deck, are found several miles away at the refuge's Environmental Education Center, near the town of Alviso; call for directions, which are complicated, or pick up a map at the visitor center. Another, less-used portion of the refuge (with one trail) is across the Dumbarton Bridge near the town of Redwood City, on the western side of San Francisco Bay.

The refuge offers two-hour weekend family nature hikes (call or check the Web site for a schedule) as well as summer day camps and an annual Kids' Night Out, which includes campfire stories, nature walks, and stargazing programs. But the real treat is what you'll see here just about any day of the year.

EATS FOR KIDS
Some picnic facilities lie along the Tidelands Trail near the visitor center, and a few picnic tables are adjacent to the education center, but you must pack out your trash. For information about **Ardenwood Pizza and Games** and other restaurants near the visitor center, see #64.

KEEP IN MIND Especially if you're coming all the way from San Francisco, you might want to combine a visit here with other family-friendly attractions in the area. Ardenwood Historic Farm (see #64) is a living-history treasure only a mile or so away. Also nearby is a nice East Bay park, Coyote Hills (Patterson Ranch Rd., Fremont, tel. 510/636–1684), which has picnic facilities, wetlands (including a marsh boardwalk), naturalist programs, and hiking and biking trails. Try the 3½-mile Bay View Trail.

SAN FRANCISCO FIRE DEPART-MENT MUSEUM

If your kids have ever dreamed of being firefighters, bring them to this small museum in Pacific Heights crammed full of fire-fighting memorabilia. Brave firefighters have been battling blazes in San Francisco for more than 150 years, and the museum traces their colorful history, from Gold Rush days through the 1906 earthquake to more modern times.

Glass cases display artifacts ranging from helmets and ribbons to buckets and uniforms. There's also an array of old photos and press clippings from famous fires and tributes to fire chiefs and Lillie Coit (*see* #48), the city's number-one fire buff. But it's the antique firefighting equipment that most fascinates kids. The city was growing rapidly during the Gold Rush in 1850, when a dozen or so rowdy volunteer fire-fighting groups first banded together to try to save the town's shack-like residences from burning down. Among their equipment were hand pumps that required up to 16 men to operate; one, built prior to 1849, is on display here. A few years later, the fire-fighting teams were professionals,

KEEP IN MIND Ask the museum's volunteer guide if it's okay to peek inside the real fire station (No. 10) next door. Chances are, if the fire bells aren't ringing just then, you and your kids can get permission to look around and see the latest in fire-fighting technology.

HEY, KIDS! Did you know that San Francisco has had to rebuild itself seven times after big fires? Six of those fires took place in Gold Rush days, about 150 years ago. But the seventh and greatest was after the 1906 earthquake, when firefighters had to battle blazes around the city without water, because the earthquake had destroyed all the water mains. Instead, firefighters used axes and dynamite to tear down buildings and build fire walls to halt the spread of the flames. It took them three whole days, but they finally stopped the blazes and saved the city.

but they still dragged hose carts themselves (being too macho to use horses); you can see one of those, too. An 1893 La France steam engine on wheels, also on display, helped replace the hand-drawn hose carts. Later engine models from 1897 and 1913 are on exhibit, too.

It's easy to overlook some little gems here, among them an original fire bell from Portsmouth Square (in Chinatown), which rang for the last time on April 18, 1906—the day of the great San Francisco earthquake and fire. Another is a small exhibit about the city's 150-year-old firebox alarm system, which operated essentially like a telegraph. Now here's the kicker: The system is still in use, with hundreds of the alarm boxes remaining on the streets. Except these days, since almost all fires are reported by phone, the boxes usually ring false alarms (school kids take note). It's just one of the tidbits waiting to be discovered at this memorial to some of the city's hottest times.

EATS FOR KIDS Just down the street from the museum, **Ella's** (500 Presidio Ave., tel. 415/441–5669) serves classic American cooking, including great pancake breakfasts and meat-loaf dinners, amid casual but attractive surroundings. Around the corner in the Laurel Village shopping plaza, **Miz Brown's** (3401 California St., tel. 415/752–2039) sports an old-fashioned soda fountain and serves breakfast all day along with burgers, fries, and shakes. Also at Laurel Village is **Pasta Pomodoro** (3611 California St., tel. 415/831–0900), which turns out tasty, inexpensive pasta dishes.

SAN FRANCISCO MAIN LIBRARY

The city's top library, which moved into a new building in 1996, can be quite entertaining, starting with the talking elevators. As you ride, a voice calls out helpful information like "going up," "please turn right," and "first floor." But then libraries are full of helpful information, and this is one of the most technologically advanced in the country. It has some 300 computer terminals, many with free Internet access and CD-ROM capability; sizable video and music collections; and, of course, a good many books. You can enjoy all this in an architecturally striking, modern building that's airy and light and has plenty of open space.

At the Fisher Children's Center, on the second floor, librarians expect kids to be noisy, and the atmosphere is anything but stuffy. Here you'll find the Electronic Discovery Center, loaded with computers where your children can read stories or play video games. If you fear they'll do too much of the latter at the expense of the former, you may accompany them to explore what's available. Each child is allowed one 30-minute session per day, and then they have

EATS FOR KIDS The small but pleasant **Library Café** (tel. 415/437–4838), on the lower level, has sandwiches, salads, and soups at reasonable prices. **Max's Opera Café** (601 Van Ness Ave., tel. 415/771–7300) serves sandwiches and other meals with portions big enough for a small family to share. Don't be surprised if your server, who may be an aspiring opera singer, breaks into song in the evening. **Vietnam II Restaurant** (701 Larkin St., tel. 415/885–1274) has inexpensive Vietnamese noodle soups and rice plates in casual surroundings. The area can be a bit questionable at night but it's fine for a lunchtime excursion.

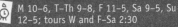

to go on a waiting list for another 30 minutes.

Connected to the Electronic Discovery Center is a big children's reading and story room. On Saturday mornings at 11, story times for families of preschoolers last about ½ hour. In another room, your kids can watch scheduled movies and learn crafts. Teenagers should check out the third-floor Teen Center, where books are geared to their age group. Elsewhere, you'll find collections of San Francisco memorabilia, an African-American Center, an Asian-American Center, and special art and photo exhibitions. A roof garden and terrace on the sixth floor is for all to use. If you want your family to get a sense of what's where, take one of the thrice-weekly tours, most suitable for fourth graders and up. But as soon as your kids spot the computers and other enticements here, they may want to desert the tour anyway. It's a place where they'll quickly discover that learning can be fun.

HEY, KIDS! The library offers all kinds of free programs for kids. You can watch a magician or a movie or learn hip-hop dancing, Japanese drumming, or Mexican paper cutting. There are also celebrations and festivals centered on different cultures. Ask the librarian for a schedule.

KEEP IN MIND Across the street in the Civic Center Plaza, a playground for elementary schoolkids, contains tire swings, slides, and monkey bars. It's a good stop after your little one has been quiet and still in the library for too long. City Hall, with its gleaming copper dome, is across the plaza and now houses the Museum of the City of San Francisco (tel. 415/928–0289), in the South Light Court. Open weekdays 8–8, it has nice exhibits about San Francisco's earthquakes and other historic city events.

SAN FRANCISCO MUSEUM OF MODERN ART

It's true that few kids (or parents, for that matter) can tell abstract expressionism from analytical cubism, or surrealism from op art. And as for Dada, he's with Mama. But children are often drawn to the frequently bright colors, abstract figures, and geometric shapes of 20th-century art. The San Francisco Museum of Modern Art—or SF-MOMA—is now the country's second-largest modern art museum.

Opened in 1995 across from the Yerba Buena Center for the Arts, the bright, airy, six-story museum is topped by a 145-foot-tall skylight tower. The permanent collections—15,000 pieces, only a small portion of them displayed at one time—highlight painting and sculpture from 1900 to 1970. Picasso, Braque, Klee, Dalí, Matisse, Pollock, de Kooning, Rivera, and Kahlo are all here. Architecture and design, 20th-century photography (by Man Ray and Ansel Adams, among others), and special exhibits are also featured, along with video, audio, and interactive media installations—ranging from "weird" to "awesome" in the words of some young visitors. Computer screens scattered about the museum

KEEP IN MIND As the museum acknowledges, some artworks have "challenging content or explicit imagery" and may not be appropriate for children. If this is a concern for you, preview the museum yourself before bringing the kids. That way, you'll know which rooms (if any) to avoid.

EATS FOR KIDS Caffe Museo (tel. 415/357–4500), on the ground floor of the museum, serves soups, focaccia sandwiches, and morning pastries; it's open during museum hours, including Thursday evenings. Buca di Beppo (855 Howard St., tel. 415/543–7673) is a boisterous, fun Italian restaurant with huge portions. The biggest collection of nearby restaurants is at Yerba Buena Gardens (see #1), especially the food court area on the main floor of Metreon, where you can get everything from burritos and burgers to Asian-style noodles.

151 3rd St.

 415/357–4000, 415/357–4097
family programs; www.sfmoma.org

 $9 adults, $5 students
13 and up; Th 6–9 half-
price; 1st T of mth free

Memorial Day–Labor Day, F–T 10–6,
Th 10–9; early Sept–late May, F–T 11–
6, Th 11–9

6 and up

are designed to help kids "make sense of modern art." The Museum Store, open daily, is superb, complete with a wonderful selection of children's art books and educational toys. Your kids can try out some toys on the spot, and you can shop without paying museum admission.

SF-MOMA is committed to attracting kids and families. On the museum's twice-yearly Family Days (June and October), each adult who brings a child pays just $2, and kids, including high school students, are free. Hands-on art projects, musical performances, and gallery tours are all included. On monthly Family Studio days, families can drop in to the Koret Education Center for free, hands-on afternoon art workshops directed by guest artists. On some spring and summer Saturdays, parents and young children can explore color and form together in a program called Children's Art Studio. The seven one-hour sessions, also at the Koret Education Center, are for ages 2½–4 and 4–6. Your child may just be inspired to join a new generation of modern artists.

HEY, KIDS! Check out the *White Painting* by an artist named Robert Rauschenberg. It's not too hard to figure out why it's called that: The paint-ing's three panels are completely white. Many visitors see it and say to them-selves, "I could paint that." What do you think the artist was trying to say? Do you think it belongs in a museum? You might want to ask your Mom or Dad or someone who works at the museum what they think about it, too.

Set on 125 acres in the fog beltway out toward the ocean, this is Northern California's largest zoo, home to more than 1,000 birds and 220 species of animals. Several facilities now rank with the best in the state.

With younger kids, start at the 7-acre Children's Zoo, near the front entrance, where they can pet farm animals in the Barnyard and peer at creepy crawlies in the indoor Insect Zoo. At the Children's Zoo's new meerkat and prairie dog exhibit, kids can crawl through a prairie dog tunnel and search through a periscope for meerkat predators.

In the main zoo's Primate Discovery Center, colobus and patas monkeys, white ruffed lemurs, and macaques live and play in a spectacular bi-level setting. The interactive learning exhibits on the ground level are ideal for school-aged kids. In the Kresge Nocturnal Gallery, next door, careful searching will yield views (however dim) of lemurs and other night creatures. Children who are afraid of the dark may find this a bit spooky. A fair walk away, a three-

HEY, KIDS! The six koalas here are the second-largest colony in North America. Most koalas live in eastern Australia and spend much of their lives high up in eucalyptus trees, which works out nicely because they eat mostly eucalyptus leaves—over 2 pounds a day. Almost any other animal would get sick or die from eating eucalyptus leaves, which are poisonous, but koala stomachs are specially designed to digest them. That may be the most exciting part of their day. When they're done eating, koalas usually fall asleep in the trees and only wake up when they're ready to eat again.

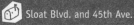 Sloat Blvd. and 45th Ave.

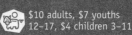 $10 adults, $7 youths 12–17, $4 children 3–11

Daily 10–5, Children's Zoo daily 11–4

415/753–7080; www.sfzoo.com

All ages

generation family of lowland gorillas lives in spacious Gorilla World—one of the most luxurious such exhibits anywhere. On Penguin Island, dozens of Magellanic penguins dive into a 200-foot pool; the penguins are fed daily at 3. In the Australian Walkabout, kangaroos and wallabies hop about, and in Koala Crossing, koalas cling shyly to the trees.

There are even non-animal activities here. Your kids can ride the carousel or the Little Puffer miniature steam train (each $2), and check out the playground near the Children's Zoo. The Wildlife Theater stages shows late June–Labor Day, Tuesday–Sunday, and the narrated Safari Train circles the zoo ($2.50 adults, $1.50 children 3–17). But the real reason to come is the animals, including a parcel of rare and endangered species. Where else in San Francisco can you see black rhinos, orangutans, ocelots, and jaguars? Not to mention lions and tigers and bears . . . oh my!

EATS FOR KIDS The zoo has four casual cafés, including the **Plaza Cafe,** just up the hill from the carousel, and the **Playfield Cafe,** near the playground and Children's Zoo, where you can get hot dogs, ice cream, and the like. After you're done at the zoo, head toward the ocean a bit to find **John's Ocean Beach Cafe** (2898 Sloat Blvd., tel. 415/665–8292), which serves breakfast all day as well as lunches of burgers, sandwiches, omelets, and soups. **Leon's Bar-B-Q** (see #42) is another option.

KEEP IN MIND
If you and your family are San Francisco residents, you qualify for sizeable discounts on zoo admission. Adults get $2 off, youths $3.50 off, and children $2.50 off. Be sure to bring a picture ID that has your address written on it.

SANTA CRUZ BEACH BOARD-WALK

9

S et alongside a wide, sandy beach about 75 miles south of San Francisco, the Santa Cruz Beach Boardwalk is the largest full-scale seaside amusement park remaining on the West Coast. Operating since 1907, it now draws 3 million visitors annually. It's a place where you can come and go as you please—strolling down the boardwalk is free—and pay for rides as you take them. Unlike many modern theme parks, the atmosphere is far from antiseptic; carnival-style games and food stands selling corn dogs and cotton candy add an air of old-fashioned funkiness and nostalgia.

For kids, though, the big draw is rides, rides, and more rides, 34 in all, some appropriate for every age group past infant. Kids ages 8 and above, and brave younger ones, head for the Giant Dipper, a classic wooden coaster that's been declared a National Historic Landmark. Less-adventurous kids can cut their coaster teeth on the smaller Sea Serpent. The Haunted Castle, a dark ride where monsters jump out at you as you pass, is relatively tame but could frighten tots. The Logger's Revenge, a log flume ride with a steep plunge at the

HEY, KIDS!

How many people have ridden the Giant Dipper roller coaster since 1924? More than 49 million—and if you ride it, maybe you'll be the 50 millionth! Though it's the seventh-oldest coaster in the country, it's often ranked among the world's top 10 by roller-coaster fans.

KEEP IN MIND From mid-May through October, you can ride to the Beach Boardwalk and back on the Santa Cruz Big Trees & Pacific Railway, which operates on a historic track that runs through Henry Cowell Redwoods State Park, down a scenic river gorge, across a 1909 steel truss bridge, and through an 1875 tunnel. Trains leave from Roaring Camp, 6 miles north of Santa Cruz in Felton, or you can start at the boardwalk. Either way, riding time is one hour. Call 831/335–4484 or visit the Web site at www.roaringcamp.com for prices and schedules.

end, is a good way to get wet on a hot day. Bumper cars and a Ferris wheel are other favorites, as is the Sky Glider, an overhead chair lift that travels high over the park. The height could scare young kids. Tots who want to avoid all of the above can take a spin on the ornate 1911 Looff carousel, with its 73 hand-carved horses. Nine kiddie rides, including Jet Copters, Sea Dragons, and Kiddie Bumper Boats, add to the fun.

You can even find entertainment here on rainy days. The boardwalk's indoor attractions include a two-story minigolf course complete with talking pirates, firing cannons, and an erupting volcano. But the main action is outdoors, where salt fills the air, waves crash in the background, and you feel like you've entered a time warp back to an old-time seaside carnival.

EATS FOR KIDS Some 30 food vendors line the boardwalk, dispensing treats such as corn dogs, pizza, burgers, nachos, funnel cake, Dippin' Dots (ice cream), garlic fries, clam chowder, and saltwater taffy. If you're in search of a sit-down place, head for the **Dolphin Restaurant** (tel. 831/426–5830), at the end of the Municipal Pier near the boardwalk. It serves seafood lunches and dinners (along with big breakfasts) amid casual decor and water views. A kids' menu includes fish-and-chips and, of course, corn dogs.

SIX FLAGS MARINE WORLD

The theme of this ambitious combination wildlife park, oceanarium, and amusement park, all packed into 160 acres about 35 miles northeast of San Francisco, is "wildlife and wild rides." So if your children want to feed a giraffe, commune with dolphins, or ride a roller coaster, they can do it here. Though amusement-park rides have recently become a big part of the scene, Marine World's traditional mainstays are its entertaining and informative shows.

The Dolphin Harbor stadium provides a slick showcase for bottle-nosed dolphins, who jump 20 feet out of the water and do tail walks, flips, air spins, and other "behaviors" (what we used to call "tricks"). If you crave more interaction, the new two-hour Dolphin Discovery program, for ages 9 and up, allows you to meet and greet dolphins in the water; it's given weekends only, will set you back a hefty $100 a person (which includes park admission), and requires reservations (tel. 707/556–5274.) The Tiger Island Splash Attack provides an underwater view of a dozen Bengal tigers at play. In other shows, sea lions do high dives, elephants demonstrate their agility, birds swoop and squawk, and daring two-legged

KEEP IN MIND A few tips can make your visit cheaper and smoother. If you buy your tickets in advance at area Longs Drugstores, you can get substantial discounts on adult fares and not have to wait through long entrance lines. If you plan to visit more than once per year, a season pass ($70–$80) can save big bucks. When you arrive, pick up a daily schedule, and plan your itinerary to make sure you cover as many shows, rides, and attractions as you can fit in. The shows are offered at various times throughout the day, and good seats often go early.

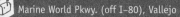

mammals perform stunts on water skis and do 32-foot free falls. In all but the human shows, trainers lace the entertainment with lessons on how animals survive—and are endangered—in the wild.

Animal exhibits include the riveting Shark Experience, where you'll move along a ramp through a clear tunnel in a huge shark tank. At Giraffe Dock, your kids can hand-feed the giraffes. At Elephant Encounter, they can play tug-of-war with an elephant; you can also ride elephants for an extra fee.

Scattered throughout the park, assorted non-animal rides range from the V-2 Vertical Velocity—which travels forward, backward, and up and down two 150-foot-tall sky towers at 70 mph—to a Ferris wheel and a river-rapids ride. Looney Tunes Seaport is a fun zone geared to kids, with rides that include a children's roller coaster and a mini–swinging ship.

HEY, KIDS! At the dolphin show, you might get picked to get kissed by a dolphin. Some other shows also pick kids to touch the animals. If you aren't chosen, there's still hope: Trainers walk around the park with camels, llamas, or reindeer and may let you touch one then.

EATS FOR KIDS Concessions at the park include **Little Italy** (for pizza) and the **Broiler** (for burgers and fries), both of which have outdoor tables. The **Carnivore Café** has ribs and chicken, and the **Lost Temple Café** features corn dogs. For dessert, the **Pink Flamingo** is the spot for flavored ices and cotton candy, and there are a number of snack stands, too. To save money, you can bring your own picnic food (no glass bottles or alcohol) to eat at tables near Lakeside Plaza and Shark Experience.

STERN GROVE FESTIVAL

Every parent knows that taking young kids to an indoor concert can be a kicking, squirming disaster. This outdoor music festival series offers a chance to introduce children to a variety of musical styles—even opera and symphony—without the worry or the cost. Sigmund Stern Grove—a 33-acre stand of eucalyptus, redwood, and fir trees in the Sunset District—provides a shady setting and natural amphitheater for the nation's oldest free outdoor concert series. It's been running each summer since 1937 and draws about 100,000 people per season.

The grove, a gift to the city from the widow of a local civic and business leader, extends down steep hillsides to a valley, where a grassy meadow looks up to a stage. Some unreserved bench seating is available directly in front of the stage; the most select seating includes picnic tables available by reservation (also free) for a maximum party of six (call 415/831–5500 at 9 AM on the Monday preceding the concert). Most of the audience stretches out or sits on the grass, while latecomers can find perches on the tree-lined hillsides

GETTING THERE Parking can be very tight near Stern Grove on concert days, so consider taking public transportation. Muni buses No. 23 and No. 28 stop at the entrance, or you can take Muni Metro streetcars K or M (exit at Sloat Blvd.).

KEEP IN MIND To pass the time while waiting for the concert, bring the Sunday paper, some toys or books for the kids, and plenty of snacks. A small playground (partially hidden by trees), just inside the 19th Avenue entrance on the Sloat Boulevard side of Stern Grove, can help entertain younger kids. And come prepared for changes in the weather as the day goes by. It's often sunny early on, so bring plenty of sunscreen. But dress everyone in layers, because Stern Grove frequently gets chilly by mid-afternoon, when the summertime fog rolls in.

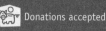

to the rear, which are decidedly less comfortable. The ideal approach is to bring a picnic lunch, arrive early (no later than noon, and by mid-morning for a good view), and spread a blanket or set low-slung lawn chairs out on the grass. Then sit back and enjoy the performance.

There are few more pleasant ways for a family to enjoy such a wide range of music and dance: Classical, opera, ballet, ethnic dance, jazz, rhythm and blues, gospel, and world music (from salsa to Celtic) are all likely to take the stage in a season. On two summer Tuesdays, the festival also offers half-day programs led by well-known artists that introduce Bay Area youngsters ages 6–10 to music, dance, and theater. Preregistration is required (tel. 415/292–2162). But whether you take advantage of these programs or just drop by on a Sunday afternoon, Stern Grove may help your kids develop a new appreciation for the performing arts.

EATS FOR KIDS Picnics are the most fun. If you don't bring food, several concession stands set up shop during the concerts, serving such items as burgers, knishes, and ice-cream bars. After the performance, head to a nearby branch of **Chevys** (3251 20th Ave., Stonestown Shopping Center, tel. 415/665–8705), serving good Tex-Mex food with children's menus. Kids can watch the tortilla-making machine. **Just Won Ton** (1241 Vicente St., tel. 415/681–2999) specializes in warming bowls of Chinese wonton soup or noodle dishes. It's small, informal, and inexpensive.

TECH MUSEUM OF INNOVATION

Loaded with custom-designed interactive exhibits, the Tech Museum is devoted solely to the innovations in microelectronics, communications, robotics, and biotechnology that have emerged in Silicon Valley. The description may be a mouthful, but this museum does a great job helping to demystify technology and make it fun for kids—and their parents. The Tech moved into a new, 132,000-square-foot, mango-and-azure domed facility in the heart of downtown in 1998. Some 250 cutting-edge exhibits are now arranged in four themed areas, and they're meant not just to inform and entertain, but to inspire museum visitors of all ages to be innovative themselves.

Activities go beyond "hands-on" to "minds-on," as museum staffers put it. In the Life Tech gallery, you and your kids can "drive" a simulated bobsled, use sound waves to "see" inside yourself, or enter images of a human body for an inside look. The Life Tech Theatre presents shows that entertainingly illuminate high-tech themes. In the Innovation gallery, you can visit a "cleanroom" to see how microchips (the stuff of Silicon Valley) are made, create your

KEEP IN MIND San Jose has other good museums for kids. One of the country's largest interactive kids' museums, the Children's Discovery Museum of San Jose (180 Woz Way, tel. 408/298–5437), whose outer walks are painted Easter-egg purple, is chock-full of hands-on exhibits geared to ages 2–12. Meanwhile, San Jose's Rosicrucian Egyptian Museum (1342 Naglee Ave., tel. 408/947–3636), housed in a building styled after an ancient temple, contains a fascinating collection of mummies (including mummified animals) and a re-created Egyptian rock tomb complete with wall paintings and hieroglyphs.

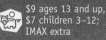
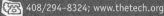
own futuristic bike design, and take an actual portrait of yourself with a laser scanner. In the Communication gallery, you and your kids can use teleconferencing equipment to communicate with one another on different floors of the museum. You can also experiment with the latest movie animation techniques and film yourself surfing, walking on the moon, or flying with Superman. And in the Exploration gallery, you can probe the ocean depths with an underwater, remote-controlled robot and test your ability to move around while weightless (as in a spaceship). The museum's Hackworth IMAX Dome Theater has a hemispherical screen 82 feet in diameter. Call for tickets or order from the Web site in advance, as demand is high.

The museum also hosts traveling exhibits that showcase state-of-the-art, experimental technologies; offers special daily programs; and has a shop stuffed with gadgets and puzzles. Maybe by the time you leave the Tech, you'll know as much as your kids do about our high-tech age.

EATS FOR KIDS

The museum's **Café Primavera** (tel. 408/885-1094) has both indoor and outdoor seating. Sandwiches, salads, pizzas, and pastas are reasonably priced. Nearby, at the landmark Fairmont Hotel, the **Fountain at the Fairmont** (170 S. Market St., tel. 408/998-1900) serves breakfast, lunch, and dinner; casual dress is fine.

HEY, KIDS! You've probably heard about Silicon Valley, where America's computer industry was born. It's been called the most inventive place on earth, and the Tech Museum is right in the heart of it. The museum was started in 1990 to showcase the latest gizmos and provide an inside look at the technology developments that usually take place behind Silicon Valley's closed doors. And just as the computer industry has grown since 1990, so has the museum; it's in a new building several times the original's size. Funny, though—computers keep getting smaller.

TILDEN PARK

Tilden Park is the East Bay's answer to San Francisco's Golden Gate Park. With more than 2,000 acres, it's about twice the size of its better-known cousin across the bay, and its grassy lawns, rolling hills, and eucalyptus and pine groves are full of recreation and picnic areas. Two lakes and peaks that rise to nearly 2,000 feet add form to the landscape. Woodsy hiking and biking trails lead throughout, and family attractions dot the park.

Tilden is particularly strong on activities for younger kids. At the Little Farm, kids can pet and feed sheep, rabbits, cows, pigs, and pygmy goats. The farm has a little barn and windmill, and there's a duck pond nearby. It's open 8:30–3:30 daily and costs nothing. Elsewhere in the park, you'll find a pony ride concession; a 1911 antique Herschel-Spillman merry-go-round, with hand-carved animals and a calliope; and the Tilden Park Steam Train, which chugs along a scenic ridge. These are open on weekends and during school vacations.

Families with kids of any age can enjoy the park's Lake Anza, which has a sandy beach

EATS FOR KIDS The park has numerous picnic areas, as well as concession stands at Lake Anza, the merry-go-round, and other locations. For information about **Fat Apple's** (a burger place) and **Cha Am** (a Thai restaurant), see #35.

HEY, KIDS! You may see the Brazilian Building in its current location near Lake Anza. The building got its name because it housed Brazil's exhibit at the 1939–40 world's fair, held on Treasure Island. Where's Treasure Island? You'll go right past it if you cross the Bay Bridge. Until recently, the island was a naval base and closed to the public, but now you and your family can take the Treasure Island exit about halfway across the bridge and drive around. You'll get some great views of San Francisco—but no sign of Long John Silver or his treasure.

that's popular for swimming (May–October). The water is generally sun warmed and sheltered from the wind by hills, and lifeguards are on duty in season. You can also fish in the lake throughout the year.

The park's eastern edge is well suited to families with older children. Here the East Bay Skyline National Recreation Trail winds along the crests of hills to Inspiration Point. The trail is accessible to hikers, horseback riders, and cyclists (the latter on fire road portions only) and links Tilden to other regional parks. Views stretch across the metropolitan Bay Area. Tilden also contains an 18-hole public golf course and driving range and a botanic garden featuring the world's most complete collection of native California plants. Just like Golden Gate Park across the bay, Tilden is the kind of place you can return to again and again and still not see it all.

KEEP IN MIND The park's Environmental Education Center (tel. 510/525–2233), near the Little Farm, offers hiking, nature, and other special programs for kids and families year-round. You can study the life of a pond, learn how to make sushi, or attend a free concert. Some programs require reservations, and some require fees (usually $5–$25), so drop by or call for a schedule. The Environmental Education Center also has an interactive exhibit about nearby Wildcat Creek (just north of Tilden) that kids might enjoy.

WATERWORLD USA

4

Though summer days are often cool and foggy in San Francisco, they can get positively scorching in Concord, 45 minutes or so to the east. And that's exactly where you'll find the water park nearest the city. Run by the Six Flags company, Waterworld USA encompasses 20 acres of places to splash, slide, float, plunge, and dip.

Ten major rides and attractions cater to kids of all ages older than infants. On the Big Kahuna, the park's most popular slide, the entire family (up to six people) can shoot its way down on a raft. Toddlers and other tots head to Treasure Island, an interactive structure featuring waterfalls, fountains, water cannons, minislides, and tire swings. Wild Water Kingdom, a 20,000-square-foot activity pool, is the other big gathering place for preschoolers, with the Dragon's Tail slide complex in Tot Town and a lily pad walk.

Older kids also find excitement at Wild Water Kingdom thanks to the Diablo Falls Shotgun Slides, which end with a 6-foot free fall into a 10-foot-deep pool. Kids have to be 48" tall

EATS FOR KIDS No coolers, food, or beverages can be brought into the park (except for infants). You can, however, have lunch in a public picnic area on the northeast end of the parking lot and return to the park if you get your hand stamped. The park's concession stands include the **Windjammer Food Court,** which sells hot dogs, cheeseburgers, and curly fries, and the **Surf Side Grill,** which serves up Mexican meals and snacks. There's also an ice-cream shop and a candy cabana.

1950 Waterworld Pkwy. (off I–680), Concord

 925/609–9283 recording, 925/609–1364
voice; www.sixflags.com/wwconcord

 $25 48" and up,
$18 47" and under,
3 and under free

 Mid-May–Sept, days and hrs vary
(mid-June–Aug, daily)

3 and up

to ride this one, as they do on several others, including the Cliff Hanger, another slide that ends in a free fall. The Typhoon Double Tube Slides, on which you travel 4½ stories down four different slides, may be even more thrilling. On the equally high Honolulu Halfpipe, daring kids can ride a towering wave both forward and backward. Less-daring kids, and parents, can float leisurely on a tube down the Kaanapali Kooler, a 15-foot-wide, 1,000-foot-long river, or body surf or ride a tube through the waves at the huge Breaker Beach Wave Pool. Free life jackets are provided, as they are at Wild Water Kingdom.

The park emphasizes safety, but accidents do happen—so keep a close eye on your kids, keep them lathered in sunscreen, and make sure youngsters stay out of the line of fire of cannonballing teens. Then prepare to get wet—very, very wet.

HEY, KIDS! Wondering about some of those ride names? They're Hawaiian. Honolulu, on Oahu island, is Hawaii's biggest city; Kaanapali is a popular beach area on the island of Maui. And the Big Kahuna? That's from a Hawaiian word for medicine man, wizard, or expert in any profession.

KEEP IN MIND You'll need to bring your own towels, and don't forget to pack dry clothes, sunscreen, sunglasses, hats, and beach shoes or sandals. You might also want to bring water toys for young kids. The park has a shop for purchasing such items, but not at bargain prices. If you arrive before the early afternoon crush, you'll stand a better chance of finding a parking space and a lounge chair for relaxing in sun or shade when you're not in the pools.

WELLS FARGO HISTORY MUSEUM

A museum off a bank lobby? Though that's a bit unusual, this little museum is well worth a detour to the Financial District. Wells Fargo began banking and express operations in San Francisco in 1852, just after the Gold Rush of 1849 lured thousands of treasure-seekers to California. The company delivered letters, safeguarded money and valuables, and bought, sold, and transported gold.

In 1861, the company ran the fabled Pony Express between Sacramento and Salt Lake City as part of the Pony Express's 10-day mail-delivery service between San Francisco and Missouri (about the same time it takes today!). The cost was 10¢ per ½ ounce (as opposed to 3¢ for a letter through the U.S. mail). By the late 1860s, Wells Fargo stagecoaches dominated overland mail and transportation in the West. So although the museum is in part a commercial for the West's oldest bank, it also documents a colorful slice of California history.

KEEP IN MIND Though the Financial District, where the museum is located, isn't exactly a family mecca, it's an easy walk from both Chinatown and the Embarcadero (see #50 and #46), so you can combine a visit here with some sightseeing in those neighborhoods. The museum is also near the California Street cable car line.

EATS FOR KIDS Monte's Eatz (404 Montgomery St., tel. 415/956–6297), an inexpensive deli and coffee shop that's right next to the museum, serves breakfast, and, at lunch, a variety of hot and cold sandwiches and Mexican food; it closes by mid-afternoon. **Clown Alley** (Jackson St. and Columbus Ave., tel. 415/421–2540), a few blocks away, stays open through dinner. It specializes in hamburgers and has both indoor and outdoor tables. For restaurants in nearby Chinatown, such as **New Asia, Pearl City,** and **Great Eastern,** see #50.

 420 Montgomery St.

 Free

M–F 9–5

 415/396–2619;
www.wellsfargohistory.com/museums

6 and up

Nicely presented exhibits cover two floors. As you enter, you'll see the 1867 Wells Fargo and Company Overland Stage Coach, one of 10 passenger coaches used in the company's route from the Bay Area to St. Louis. Payment got each of nine tightly packed passengers a "through-ticket and 15 inches of seat." Nearby, you'll find a re-created early-day Wells Fargo office—complete with telegraph (you can send messages back and forth between two desks using Morse Code), agent's desk, documents, treasure boxes, and package scales. Other exhibits focus on stagecoach drivers, the bandit-poet known as Black Bart, the Pony Express, and the Gold Rush. On the second floor, your kids can climb on a cutaway stagecoach seat, take the reins, and play driver. Nearby sits a coach (without wheels) that the entire family can squeeze into to get a feel for just how cramped—and no doubt hot and sticky—it got inside. There's also a first-floor general store where you can pick up souvenirs, such as gold-panning kits and model stagecoaches. The only thing you can't do is send a letter for 10¢.

HEY, KIDS! Black Bart, who has his own exhibit here, was the most feared outlaw of his day. Between 1877 and 1883, he is believed to have held up close to 30 stagecoaches in the California Gold Country, dressing in black and waving his shotgun at the drivers and passengers. Nobody knew who he was, since he always wore a mask. Then one day he was caught. When they ripped off his mask, he turned out to be a well-known San Francisco businessman, who never even loaded his gun.

WINCHESTER MYSTERY HOUSE

Sarah Winchester's 160-room Victorian dwelling in San Jose is touted as the "world's oddest historical mansion," and you won't get many arguments on that. A wealthy widow—she was heiress to the Winchester rifle fortune—and devotee of the occult, Winchester began work on her house in 1884. After her husband and baby daughter died, Winchester apparently was convinced by a spiritualist that continuous building would appease the spirits of those killed by Winchester firearms and win eternal life for herself. That plan failed—she eventually died at age 82—but it certainly kept a platoon of carpenters employed. Following no discernible blueprints, they worked on the mansion 24 hours a day for the next 38 years, ending with her death in 1922.

The results are both beautiful and bizarre: Rooms with Tiffany glass windows, gold and silver chandeliers, inlaid doors, and parquet floors are juxtaposed with stairways and chimneys that lead nowhere, doors that open to blank walls, windows that are built into floors, and a layout so rambling and complex that the guides quip, "If you get separated

EATS FOR KIDS You can relax after the tour at the **Winchester Café,** within the Mystery House, which serves snacks, desserts, and drinks. For good Mexican food, including fajitas with fresh tortillas as well as special kids' menus, check out the nearby branch of **Chevys** (550 S. Winchester Blvd., tel. 408/241–0158). The **Florentine** (745 S. Winchester Blvd., tel. 408/243–4040) has reasonably priced, traditional Italian food, such as pastas and pizzas, and a children's menu. For more San Jose restaurants, see #6.

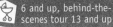
from the group, there's no guarantee you'll ever be found." Even Winchester and her servants used maps to get around the bewildering maze.

The standard tour, a 1½-mile trek, lasts one hour, hitting the highlights as it passes through 110 rooms. A 55-minute, behind-the-scenes tour, good for return visitors, reveals the previously unseen workings of the estate, including the stables, a basement, and an unfinished ballroom. The downside of the latter tour for families is that kids under 13 aren't allowed on it for safety reasons (you have to wear hard hats, too). You can also take self-guided tours of the extensive Victorian gardens and firearms museum, devoted mainly to the Winchester rifle, the "gun that won the West." The Mystery House also hosts special spooky "flashlight tours" on the evenings of Halloween and Friday the 13th. These cost extra but are led by real ghosts. Just kidding—or ARE we?

HEY, KIDS! While on the tour, see how many of the house's 10,000 windows, 467 doorways, 367 steps, 52 sky-lights, 47 fireplaces, 40 bedrooms, 40 staircases, 17 chimneys, 6 kitchens, and 3 elevators you can count. You might want to bring your calculator. But where are the bathrooms?

KEEP IN MIND Very young kids could get restless during the hour-long tour, and that presents some problems: Since you aren't allowed to wander on your own—you'd get lost—there's no way to bail out. Also note that strollers can't be accommodated; there are simply too many stairways and narrow passages. But for school-age kids and up, the tour can be remarkably compelling. The narration isn't confined to stuffy descriptions of house and family; it's jaunty and, like the tour itself, covers a lot of ground.

YERBA BUENA GARDENS

Once a bleak industrial area, the South of Market blocks around—and above—the Moscone Convention Center have been transformed into a showplace of arts facilities, parks, and entertainment, all called Yerba Buena Gardens. Thanks to recent additions, it's now a premier family playground.

Long talked about and long in the making, the Rooftop at Yerba Buena Gardens occupies 10 acres atop the largely underground Moscone Center South. The Rooftop, reached via a pedestrian bridge over Howard Street from the northern section of Yerba Buena Gardens, is loaded with activities geared to kids, though parents can play, too. A restored 1906-vintage Looff carousel, from the long-defunct Playland-at-the-Beach, is back in action. At the Zeum, a high-tech interactive arts center, kids can create animation or a multimedia video. An NHL-size Ice Skating Center is San Francisco's only year-round public rink. Also here are a bowling alley and three landscaped acres with a Children's Garden and Play Circle, including a stream, slides, and child-size hedge maze.

KEEP IN MIND Yerba Buena Gardens has some nice grassy spaces to just sit and relax. Best is the Esplanade, above Moscone Center North, which also has a terrace with outdoor cafés. The Martin Luther King Jr. Memorial Fountain includes a wide waterfall that children can scamper behind.

EATS FOR KIDS **Mo's Gourmet Hamburgers** (adjacent to Zeum, tel. 415/957–3779), an outpost of a North Beach restaurant, has some outdoor tables. Metreon has several good eateries. **In the Night Kitchen** is an American diner with a Maurice Sendak theme and a fourth-floor view. Within the bustling first-floor food court, **Long Life Noodle Company** specializes in Asian-style noodles, and **Luna Azul** serves up burritos, quesadillas, and nachos. Other restaurants in the food court feature burgers, sushi, or desserts. For **Buca di Beppo**, a nearby Italian restaurant, see #11.

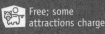
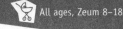
The Metreon, a futuristic Sony Entertainment Center, is adjacent to the parklands above Moscone Center North. It contains an IMAX theater along with 15 regular movie screens, plus an array of shops and restaurants. Three interactive attractions based on literary works are geared to families. In the play space inspired by Maurice Sendak's *Where the Wild Things Are,* children encounter goblins, a hall of mirrors, and a 17-foot-tall Wild Thing. *Airtight Garage,* based on the work of French graphic novelist Jean "Moebius" Giraud, features a host of electronic and virtual-reality games, including a virtual bowling alley. And in the area based on David Macauley's *The Way Things Work,* your kids can view a three-screen, three-dimensional show illustrating how mechanical things work—and sometimes don't—with bubbles, smoke, and blasts of air and water. Access to all three costs $17 ages 13 and up, $13 children 3–12. It's all fun, but you don't have to spend that kind of money to keep kids happy here. You'll find plenty of alternatives at this diverse, family-friendly entertainment complex.

HEY, KIDS! The city of San Francisco itself was called Yerba Buena from the time it was settled in the late 1700s until 1847. In Spanish, Yerba Buena means "good herb," which probably referred to a type of mint that grew here. When the city began to grow, just before the Gold Rush of 1849, the name was changed to San Francisco, after St. Francis of Assisi. But for many years after the Gold Rush, the city was anything but saintly—it had a wild and rowdy reputation.

CLASSIC GAMES

"I SEE SOMETHING YOU DON'T SEE AND IT IS BLUE." Stuck for a way to get your youngsters to settle down in a museum? Sit them down on a bench in the middle of a room and play this vintage favorite. The leader gives just one clue—the color—and everybody guesses away.

"I'M GOING TO THE GROCERY..." The first player begins, "I'm going to the grocery and I'm going to buy... " and finishes the sentence with the name of an object, found in grocery stores, that begins with the letter "A." The second player repeats what the first player has said, and adds the name of another item that starts with "B." The third player repeats everything that has been said so far and adds something that begins with "C" and so on through the alphabet. Anyone who skips or misremembers an item is out (or decide up front that you'll give hints to all who need 'em). You can modify the theme depending on where you're going that day, as "I'm going to X and I'm going to see..."

FAMILY ARK Noah had his ark—here's your chance to build your own. It's easy: Just start naming animals and work your way through the alphabet, from antelope to zebra.

PLAY WHILE YOU WAIT

NOT THE GOOFY GAME Have one child name a category. (Some ideas: first names, last names, animals, countries, friends, feelings, foods, hot or cold things, clothing.) Then take turns naming things that fall into that category. You're out if you name something that doesn't belong in the category—or if you can't think of another item to name. When only one person remains, start again. Choose categories depending on where you're going or where you've been—historic topics if you've seen a historic sight, animal topics before or after the zoo, upside-down things if you've been to the circus, and so on. Make the game harder by choosing category items in A-B-C order.

DRUTHERS How do your kids really feel about things? Just ask. "Would you rather eat worms or hamburgers? Hamburgers or candy?" Choose serious and silly topics—and have fun!

BUILD A STORY "Once upon a time there lived..." Finish the sentence and ask the rest of your family, one at a time, to add another sentence or two. Bring a tape recorder along to record the narrative—and you can enjoy your creation again and again.

GOOD TIMES GALORE

WIGGLE & GIGGLE Give your kids a chance to stick out their tongues at you. Start by making a face, then have the next person imitate you and add a gesture of his own—snapping fingers, winking, clapping, sneezing, or the like. The next person mimics the first two and adds a third gesture, and so on.

JUNIOR OPERA During a designated period of time, have your kids sing everything they want to say.

THE QUIET GAME Need a good giggle—or a moment of calm to figure out your route? The driver sets a time limit and everybody must be silent. The last person to make a sound wins.

HIGH FIVES

BEST IN TOWN
Alcatraz Island
Point Reyes National Seashore
Chinatown
Exploratorium
Golden Gate Park

BEST OUTDOORS
Point Reyes National Seashore

WACKIEST
Winchester Mystery House

BEST CULTURAL ACTIVITY
Chinatown

NEW & NOTEWORTHY
Yerba Buena Gardens

BEST MUSEUM
Exploratorium

SOMETHING FOR EVERYONE

ALL AROUND TOWN

MANY THANKS!

To my parents, Clark and Mary Norton, with loving thanks, who introduced me to San Francisco when I was 9. For providing invaluable information, assistance, and suggestions for this book, the author would like to thank Laurie Armstrong; Helen Chang; Timothy Chanaud; David Perry; Susan Wilson; Jan Bollwinkel-Smith; Al Sassus; Nick and Esther Baran; Mel, Emily, and Natalie Flores; Mimi Sarkisian; Pat and Anne Forte; Michael and Beth Ward; Michael and Mary Reiter; Veronica Daly; Sheldon Clark; Tom and Chris Sonnemann; Bob Siegel; Pat Koren; Mary Viviano; Lana Beckett; and my most faithful researchers and travel companions, Catharine, Grael, and Lia Norton.

I'm also grateful to my ever-supportive and instructive editors at Fodor's, with special thanks to Andrea Lehman.

Clark Norton

the end.